Reveal their favorite restaurants,
coffee bars, and secret spots

ROME

ROME

100 Locals in Rome
Reveal their favorite restaurants, coffee bars, and secret spots

ISBN: 978-1-940387-04-8

www.onehundredlocals.com

Reveal their favorite restaurants,
coffee bars, and secret spots

DON'T BE A TOURIST, BE A ROMAN

We live in a world where every product or service you may want to purchase has already been reviewed online by thousands of satisfied and frustrated clients alike. From a toothbrush to a car, our consumer decisions have never been better informed. Yet, when it comes to travel and leisure in foreign destinations, there is a huge knowledge gap of how the locals live and play.

In a city like Rome, renowned for breathtaking open spaces, rich culinary traditions, and a formidable coffee culture, do you really want to follow the herds to the same-old tired places, infested with pretend gladiators and street vendors, to eat mediocre pasta at dingy tourist traps, and pay triple for a watery cappuccino?

In this new crowd-sourced guide of the eternal city, 100 Romans share with you their secret spots, their top restaurants, and their favorite bars. Savvy travelers may already know some of these recommendations, but most are surprising additions you will be hard-pressed to find on the usual-suspect "trip advisory" sites.

Packed with curated suggestions of where to hang out, eat, and drink in Rome, this guide will prod you to venture beyond the epicenter of the metropolis to discover the best hidden gems of the city, known only to its insiders.

Romans love their city. They also love to play, to eat well, and to live life on the slow lane when the mind, heart, and soul require it. This book is as much a travel guide of Rome as it is a love letter to a city from citizens who are eternally enamored with where they live. Because for all the frustrations of its daily grind, Rome remains an irresistible seductress.

Whether you are a seasoned traveler to the city, a newbie, or indeed a seventh-generation Roman, prepare to discover this magical land in its truest color. A color as mesmerizing as its salmon-tinted evening lights reflecting on monuments and structures as timeless as time itself.

Contents

100 Romans
— *Reveal their local secrets*

Via
Giulia
109

Caprese
Salad
89

Credits
— *Who made me?*

Editor - *A.M. Khalifa*
Design - *Joe Scerri*
Interviews - *Shaza Saker*
Copyediting - *Sharon Baker*
Photography - *Simone Strano and Fernanda Mayer*

⭐ *indicates a local favorite that was picked more than three times.*

© 2018 Mavenhill

Special thanks to:
The City of Rome, the Vatican City, the Region of Lazio

Piazza Navona,
Rome, 6.40 am

01

Alessia Gatti

Actress and Filmmaker

— Born and bred in Rome, recommends...

Made or Born Roman?

 I was born in Fano, but moved to Rome to study at La Sapienza University."

Secret Spot
— *Il Buco*

My favorite place is what Romans call *il buco*, or the 'hole.' It's off the tourist trail, known only to true Romans. Located at the top of the Aventino hill, I wander there in the evenings to clear my thoughts. After a hike up the hill, you will reach a huge door of the Villa del Priorato di Malta, where, if you look through the keyhole, you can see the dome of St. Peter's cathedral, perfectly lit through the trees of the garden. My soul tingles every time I do that.

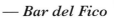 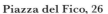

Favorite Bar
— *Bar del Fico*

Piazza del Fico, 26

I don't drink coffee, so a bar is where I get a cocktail! Bar del Fico is right behind Piazza Navona, so perfect for a night out. Few places make you feel at one with the city like this. Fortunately, this is not a touristic haunt by any stretch of the imagination. You will only find real Romans here. Whatever I have planned for the rest of the outing, the evening always starts here. If you go there, you will know why.

Favorite Restaurant
 — *Ristorante Berninetta*

Via Pietro Cavallini, 14

This is one of my favorite restaurants and you absolutely have to try the fried artichoke leaves. I love the familiar ambience and the simplicity of this place. Every dish is prepared with love and authenticity, exactly the way homemade food needs to be. You'll find all typical Roman fare like *bucatini all'amatriciana* (a traditional Italian pasta sauce based on cured pork cheek, pecorino cheese, and tomato), *spaghetti cacio e pepe* (with pecorino cheese and ground black pepper), and *saltimbocca* (veal lined with prosciutto).

What do you like most about living in Rome?

What I adore most about this city is its beauty and wealth of history and monuments. I remember when I first moved here I always took buses as my preferred mode of transport. Often my jaw would drop at the abundance of monuments, historic squares, and magic corners. But Rome is also special because of the Romans. I love their sense of humor, their honesty, and their authenticity."

Favorite Bar

— *Bar del Fico*

My secret to happiness:

"To see the glass half full rather than half empty"

Fernando Nardi

Flood Risk Expert

— Born in Abruzzo, now based in Rome, recommends...

Made or Born Roman?

 Secret Spot
— *La Fontana delle Tartarughe*

This fountain in Piazza Mattei in the Sant'Angelo district of Rome is my absolute favorite spot, even though in a magical city like Rome it's hard to narrow it down to just one. Like many special locations waiting to be discovered, this place is shrouded in history and concealed behind narrow alleys and little-heard-of monuments. It was built in the late Italian Renaissance.

Favorite Bar
— *Grecco Enjoy*

Via Gregorio VII, 239

There are many household-name bars in Rome, but my favorite is Grecco Enjoy. Go there to be treated like family by the friendly bartenders and for the most delicious cappucino you will ever taste. Mark this an essential pit-stop after your tour of St. Peter's Square.

Favorite Restaurant
— *Pizzeria da Baffetto*

Via del Governo Vecchio, 114

I have a number of restaurants I go to regularly. As you can imagine, eating well in a city like Rome is quite easy. Still, I have a particular soft spot for this pizzeria. It's quite well known so the line to get in can be daunting. Both locals and tourists in the know flock there for the excellent food. If you happen to go with a regular, as if by magic, you will find yourself ahead of the line. Welcome to Rome!

What do you like most about living in Rome?

I love that even the simplest pleasures, like a walk through the city center, are memorable. I like to start from my neighborhood near St. Peter's Cathedral, then stroll by St. Angelo Bridge, Via del Governo Vecchio, Piazza del Fico, and Piazza Navona. I stop at the Pantheon where my reward is any one of the excellent bars or restaurants in the tiny squares dotting the area around the Pantheon."

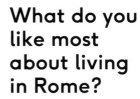

Made or Born Roman?

> *I was born in the Trastevere quarter, at the foot of the hill that has the Gianicolo at its summit. I left the city when I was six-years-old, but returned to Rome as an adult."*

🍴 Favorite Restaurant
— *Renato & Luisa*

Via dei Barbieri, 25

A small, busy restaurant in the center of Rome named after the two partners who own and run it. I go there for modern takes on traditional Roman cuisine with a healthier and vegetarian-friendly twist. Start with pralines of goat's cheese with walnuts and honey or a fish carpaccio. For your main dish, I recommend their homemade pasta with truffles or a fillet of beef with port-wine and dried prunes. Wash it down with their gorgeous house wine.

Daniela Filippin

Illustrator and Painter

— Born in Rome, raised across the world, recommends...

🔒 Secret Spot
— *Monteverde*

The Monteverde neighborhood is the closest to my heart. The area around the Gianicolo and the streets leading down to the bustling quarter of Trastevere is enchanting, taking you through the sites of the Risorgimento, the Baroque Fountain of the Acqua Paola, the sixteenth-century building occupied by the breathtaking Spanish Embassy, the church of San Pietro in Montorio, and the ultimate art history textbook staple, Bramante's Tempietto.

🍷 Favorite Bar
— *Bar Pasticceria Carini*

Via Giacinto Carini, 31

Sitting across from the public park of Villa Sciarra, this unassuming bar and pâtisserie delights with wonderful coffees and aperitifs, freshly squeezed juices, baked pastries, and cakes baked with just about any flour under the sun. They also have great alternatives to dairy milk, like soy, rice, and almond.

What do you love most about Rome?

> *Rome welcomes and feeds me and usually projects back my feelings at any given time."*

Favorite Bar
— *Bar Castroni*

Made or Born Roman?

> *I was born in the south of Italy. I moved to Rome in 1996 to study, and have since left and come back a few times, but Rome will always be my city. Most of my family still lives there."*

> *Rome was caput mundi, and you can breathe this magnificent past while walking, driving and going around every corner of the city. Rome was and will always be a source of endless beauty. I love the crowded bars. I stand there to observe how the baristas work miracles to serve the demanding customers. I have not seen this anywhere else in the world. Or the delicious Roman pizza al taglio (pizza by the slice) readily available at every nook and cranny."*

What do you like most about living in Rome?

My secret to happiness:
"Observing beauty from afar"

Federica Donato

Painter/Cultural Guide

— Born and bred in Rome, recommends...

🍴 Favorite Restaurant
— *Club Machiavelli* ⭐

Via Machiavelli, 49

This place is not too far from the Colosseum, but tucked in a hidden street in the heart of the 'real Rome.' A very warm and friendly trattoria where Mauro, the owner and chef, cooks typical Roman dishes with fresh ingredients mostly sourced from the famous Mercato dell'Esquilino off Piazza Vittorio. You must try the *tonnarelli cacio e pepe*, a traditional pasta dish made from Roman pecorino cheese and black pepper.

🔒 Secret Spot
— *La Basilica di Santa Prudenziana*

This was a domus ('house' in Latin) with ample baths that went on to become a haven for Christians when they were still being persecuted. A little known spot that's not crowded at all. I love to sit there and ponder the history of this place and this city centuries ago.

🍷 Favorite Bar
— *Bar Castroni*

Via Cola di Rienzo, 196

This is not just a bar, but a gastronomic wonderland of delicious products from various regions of Italy. After I have my espresso, I always buy new things to discover as well as grab my longtime favorites, including coarsely ground coffee—*miscela robusta*.

My secret to happiness:

"Laughing with the people I love most"

Maria Angeli

Singer/Songwriter

— *Born in Switzerland and bred in Rome, recommends...*

Made or Born Roman?

I was born in Switzerland to Roman parents, then moved back to Rome where I was raised.

🔒 Secret Spot
— *Piazza Navona*

When the sun is shining, this Roman landmark is particularly beautiful and lively. It's a symbol of the Baroque era, boasting beautiful creations of the great Francesco Bernini (Chiesa di Sant'Agnese in Agone) and Gian Lorenzo Bernini (Fontana dei Quattro Fiumi). During the warmest months, the drains of the fountains are blocked to flood the square and ease the heat.

🍷 Favorite Bar
— *Café et Caffè*

Piazza di Sant'Eustachio, 50

Across from one of the most famous bars in Rome is this tiny gem of a Neapolitan bar. Step inside to be transported to a small bar in a remote part of southern Italy. It's not fancy at all, but they specialize in Neapolitan coffee, made in the authentic way by real Neapolitans. In summer their *granita di caffè* could very well have been made with love in heaven.

🍴 Favorite Restaurant
— *Settimio All'Arancio*

Via dell'Arancio, 50

I've been going to this unassuming joint for a long time for their authentic Roman cuisine. The truffle pastas are out of this world, while their lamb dishes and the *bistecca alla Fiorentina* will have you coming back for more. But it's their unearthly desserts that will really steal your heart and seal the deal.

What do you like most about living in Rome?

I don't live in Rome all the time, I'm also based in Paris and Berlin. I find this is a good way to maintain a healthy relationship with this marvelous but often chaotic city. No matter how long I've lived here, I always discover something new hidden at the corner of a building or poking out of a rooftop. A lifetime wouldn't be enough to fully discover this amazing city that spells 'love' backwards—amor.

Secret Spot
— Lago dell'EUR

You could do a lot worse in life than cycle around the Park in the EUR neighborhood. I have very fond childhood memories of playing here and feeding the ducks. It has a man-made lake that's surprisingly charming and the center of various water activities. At the end of your ride I recommend you reward your valiant efforts with an ice cream from Giolitti.

Favorite Bar
— Mela Verde

Via Paolo di Dono, 41-45

The pastry selection has never disappointed me. They are always patient as I make up my mind about the decadence I will indulge in. It's a busy little corner of the world with plenty of suits getting their daily ration of caffeine and sugar. Their aperitif kicks at 6 p.m. and is well worth coming back for.

My secret to happiness:
"Learning to love people and use things and not the other way around"

Made or Born Roman?

" I was born in Rome, but spent 15 years in the UK before I was drawn back in 2010."

Tino Contino
Quantitative Researcher

— Born and bred in Rome, recommends...

What do you like most about living in Rome?

" The unexpected and pleasant surprises just around the corner of familiar places. Rome is full of those. Just when you think you have it all figured out, something pops up that forces you to reassess. Fortunately, in most cases, the surprises are pleasant."

Favorite Restaurant
— Agricoltura Nuova

Via Castel di Leva, 371

An organic farmhouse that sells directly to the public. Their little-known secret is that on Fridays, Saturdays, and Sundays, they have an organic restaurant and pizzeria. They serve unlimited pizza with a twist. The chefs keep churning delicious one-meter pies with the ingredients sourced from whatever is in season in the farm shop. You could have pumpkin and ricotta, or a sausage with artichoke pizza. The waiters come round serving each table a few slices. I also recommend the battered vegetables.

07

My secret to happiness:

"Surrounding myself with beautiful souls"

Sarah-Jayne Contino

Event Producer

— *Born in the UK, now based in Rome, recommends...*

 Secret Spot
—*Appia Antica*

A walk with a loved one down the Appia Antica is one of my favorite things to do. This is a great cycle path as well if you know how to avoid the worst of the cobbled parts. To think that this was one of the main trade arteries through Italy for hundreds of years, and parts of it are still used today, is just incredible. Without fail, whenever I walk or cycle here I am transported back to ancient Roman times. Very little has changed here, and it's reassuring to have this connection with history. It's always worth taking water and a hat with you as shade can be hard to come by. Mosquito repellent during summer is also not a bad idea at all.

🍴 Favorite Restaurant
— *L'Archeologia*

Via Appia Antica, 139

Once you have built an appetite from your walk on the Appia Antica, you can head to L'archeologia. We probably go once every couple of months, and every time we let the owners or the waiters guide us towards the best seasonal dishes. The menu is extensive and changes accordingly, but is distinctly Roman.

🍷 Favorite Bar
— *Caffè di Leva*

Via di Castel Di Leva, 246

This little corner bar in the piazza below my place would have to be my favorite. Their homemade *frutti di bosco* (berries) *cornetti* are divine. It's a family-run place, and the handful of tables outside become the focal point for heated discussions on current affairs, or which getaway small town to visit this weekend.

What do you like most about living in Rome?

I love the feel of the cobbled streets under my feet. Though the ground is uneven, there is still a strong sense of strength and stability beneath you. People-watching, and there is no better place than Rome to do this. Be it a newly intertwined young couple shyly getting to know each other over a gelato or an elderly couple silently sharing the shade outside their door."

Made or Born Roman?

I 'became' a Roman when I moved here from the UK at the age of 22. Learning the language was pretty tough but the biggest challenge was the culture shift."

08

My secret to happiness:

"Never sweat the small things"

Ludovica Mari

Radio Journalist

— Born and bred in Rome, recommends...

Made or Born Roman?

❝ *I was born in Rome, but lived all across Italy for the first decade of my life before returning to the city of my birth.* ❞

🔒 Secret Spot
— Piccole Sorelle Di Gesu'

In the leafy suburb of EUR, there is a little-known order of trappist monks of the Little Sisters of Jesus. Sitting inside the monastery between the trees on the austere benches provides unparalleled freedom and spirituality. When you are done, walk down the hill as you munch on the delicious trappist chocolates produced by the monks.

🍷 Favorite Bar
— Bar Andreotti

Via Ostiense, 54-56

I love having breakfast at this bar, which is also a very fancy pastry shop. For a glutton like me, this is heaven. I am not a regular, so the baristas do not prep my coffee the minute I walk in as they do with others. But service is fast and courteous nevertheless. Often you will run into local celebrities there, like the Turkish-born director Ferzan Özpetek.

🍴 Favorite Restaurant
— Le Casette di Campagna

Via Affogalasino, 40

Restaurants, cafes, and bars in a city like Rome are constantly changing and influenced by what's hip at any given moment. That said, this is one of my favorite restaurants and it seems I always end up going there because it's timeless. The complex is encased in a beautiful garden, and there are two separate eateries, a traditional pizzeria, and a full restaurant. I recommend the grilled meats and pretty much anything on the dessert menu.

What do you like most about living in Rome?

❝ *The thing I love most about living in Rome is that every day has a slight feeling of being on a holiday. The climate, the art, the beach being less than half an hour away, and the greenery. Shame this holiday is sometimes slightly tainted by the traffic! But for every Roman frustration, there is always a quick and satisfying balm to make the city worth its trouble."*

 Secret Spot
— *Via del Pellegrino*

This street is close to Campo de' Fiori. As you walk through it, you will come across a small arch, Arco degli Acetari, leading into a very tiny secluded courtyard. Take a peek inside and it will feel like you've stepped back in time, with laundry drying in the sun, aromas of delicious food wafting in the air, and the sound of silence. A perfect, peaceful oasis amidst the downtown chaos.

Favorite Bar
— *Necci*

Via Fanfulla da Lodi, 68

A stylish bar with a wraparound garden terrace. The coffee is excellent, as are the wine and spirits selections. You can't go wrong with the food served there for lunch or dinner. This has been hip since the 1960s. Pier Paolo Pasolini used to hang out here and even shot parts of his first film at this bar in 1961.

My secret to happiness:
"Understanding that life simply happens – enjoy it as it comes"

Antonio Amendola

Photographer/Philanthropist

— *Born and bred in Rome, recommends...*

What do you like most about living in Rome?

" *The multiple layers and pervasive sense of time and history. You literally see it just everywhere. Conversion of identities and cultures carved on the walls of the buildings and etched on the paved roads. After some time here, you take it for granted. But if you slow down you realize there are signs of the past everywhere begging for your attention."*

Made or Born Roman?

" *I was born in Rome but I grew up in southern Italy, on the Adriatic Sea. I returned to Rome twenty years ago to do my military service, then decided to stay here for good."*

 Favorite Restaurant
— *The Winebar at La Città del Gusto*

Via E. Fermi, 161

The Winebar is located in an ultra-modern building on the banks of the river Tiber, in the trendy and lively neighborhood of Ostiense. The entire complex of La città del Gusto is five floors and is the headquarters of Gambero Rosso where the slow food movement was born.

It houses a training school, a shop, and a kitchen stadium. The wine bar is never crowded and overlooks the city with a view of Pasolini's Rome. I like to order a platter of prosciutto, salami and northern Italian cheeses. The wine choices are astounding and affordable relative to the quality.

Favorite
Restaurant
— *Ristorante
Ditirambo*

Made or Born Roman?

> *I was born a Roman. I left the city at the age of eighteen to pursue my studies in music across the world, but have been back in the city for the past seven years."*

 Secret Spot
— *Parco degli Acquedotti*

Via Lemonia, 256

The Parco degli Acquedotti is a real hidden gem, just a few metro stops from the center. It's named after the aqueducts that go through it—on one side it is crossed by the Aqua Felix and also contains part of the Aqua Claudia and the remains of Villa delle Vignacce.

 Favorite Bar
— *BArt Auditorium Parco della Musica*

Viale Pietro De Coubertin, 30

A perfect location if you're staying for a concert or for one of the exhibits, or simply if you wish to enjoy the sun in the cavea of the Auditorium. The baristas know me by name and will always take the time to exchange a few words regardless of how busy they are.

My secret to happiness:
"To follow the music wherever it takes me and love my dear ones completely"

Fabiana Biasini

Pianist

— *Born and bred in Rome, recommends...*

What do you like most about living in Rome?

> *The weather, especially the warm Octobers when it starts getting chilly elsewhere in Europe. I love the multicolored sunsets, the 'oldness', the fresh vegetables, the free-flowing fountains, the little hidden piazzas, the endless churches, the pine trees, and the cats that roam the streets."*

 Favorite Restaurant
— *Ristorante Ditirambo*

Piazza della Cancelleria, 74-75

Luca, the owner, travels to various farms and vineyards around Italy to handpick the ingredients. We go to Ditirambo every time we have guests and want to make a *bella figura*—a good impression! My family and I love having a Sunday brunch there. Luca and the waiters know us well, and often if we are there late into the night, they'll join us for a glass of wine. My favorite dish is the *millefoglie di zucchini*—leaves of deep fried zucchini with tomato, mozzarella, and parmesan.

St. Pietro e Paolo,
Rome, 6.40 pm

11

My secret to happiness:

"Meeting friends without needing to make appointments"

Grazia del Giudice

∞∞∞ Architectural Conservator/ Interior Designer ∞∞∞

— Born and bred in Rome, recommends...

Made or Born Roman?

❝ *Roman by birth. I've lived in other parts of Italy, but always considered Rome to be my center of gravity.*❞

🔒 Favorite Spot — *Pantheon*

My favorite spot is the Pantheon, a truly magical location. I worked for ten years restoring it and know every decorative nook and cranny there, just like the body of a lover. When you've spent quality time in a place like this, you appreciate it in a different light. As it happens, it is also where I got married. I always return there when I have a need for happy memories.

🍷 Favorite Bar — *I Dolci di Checco*

Via Benedetta, 7

Although tiny with no outdoor tables, this is my absolute favorite bar, located in Trastevere right behind the fountain of Piazza Trilussa. The longtime baristas know me and my children by name and are always warm and affectionate. The pastries and gelato are delicious, and the coffee is as good as it gets in Rome. It's also a great place for a light lunch.

🍴 Favorite Restaurant — *Agustarello*

Via Giovanni Branca, 100

Located in Trastevere, this is a budget, non-pretentious, simple, family restaurant with paper tablecloths. The food is homemade. True to Roman culinary tradition, you'll find here the typical fare of the everyday man and woman. I love the fresh chicory served with olive oil and anchovies (*puntarelle*), and from their dessert menu, the *tiramisù*. When the weather is nice, their outdoor tables overlooking the square are always full. The atmosphere is always joyous and you get the feeling that everyone there knows each other.

What do you like most about living in Rome?

❝ *I love that it's always bright, with the rays of the morning sun over my neighborhood, Trastevere, beautiful and warming. That I can move around with my bicycle and never need to use my car. I love the reflection of the light and the monuments on the river, and the salmon and golden sunsets. I love having all these ancient artistic masterpieces within everyone's reach.*❞

My secret to happiness:
"To always have a positive mental attitude"

Liza Traniello

Program Coordinator

— *Born in the UK, now based in Rome, recommends...*

Made or Born Roman?

 I was born in Britain then moved to Italy. I moved to Rome in 2001 for work and have been here since."

🔒 Favorite Spot
— *Giardino degli Aranci*

Around the fourteenth century, the Savelli family built an impenetrable castle on the Aventino Hill with this enchanting park inside. Translated as the Garden of Oranges, the view from this small rectangular garden is exquisite, especially at night. There are a few places in the world that can overpower your state of mind and calm and enchant you. This is one of them.

🍸 Favorite Bar
— *Rec 23*
Piazza dell'Emporio, 1-2, Roma

Being part British, part Italian, bar means two things to me. For delicious wines, sparkling prosecco, and exciting cocktails, this is my favorite joint. You have to try their homemade crisps. Saturday brunch is great for the family—they have a kids club. For coffee bars, it's hard to find a bad one in Rome. I take mine *lungo macchiato*.

🍴 Favorite Restaurant
— *Vineria il Chianti*

Via del Lavatore, 81

Strategically located a short walk from the Trevi Fountain, this is hands down my favorite restaurant in Rome. The food is homemade delicious. Wine lovers will get tipsy just staring at their wall display. Go for the *a la carte* menu in the evening and the buffet at lunchtime. Excellent value for money.

What do you like most about living in Rome?

 I love that every corner in this city has its charm. Having lived in the UK for a while, I have also come to appreciate Rome's amazing weather. When you live here long enough, the thought of a colder climate becomes unthinkable. I love that the seasons are mild, and when we are supposed to be in the heart of winter, you get an unexpected bout of sunshine to lift your spirits."

🔒 Secret Spot
— *Teatro Marcello*

Named after Emperor Augustus's nephew, Marcello, the Teatro is sometimes referred to as the Jewish Colosseum. This ancient open-air theater located in the Rione of Sant'Angelo, is still used as a performance venue during the summer, when it comes alive with wonderful shows.

🍷 Favorite Bar
— *Meccanismo*

Piazza Trilussa, 34

Its cumbersome name apart, this place is ideal for a morning coffee on the run or a leisurely drink in the evening. In the mornings, the staff greet me by name. Having my cappuccino and cream-filled *cornetto* ready at the counter feels like I'm at home.

My secret to happiness:

"Being grateful for the simplest things I have"

Antonella Stasi

Producer

— *Born in Milan, now based in Rome, recommends...*

Made or Born Roman?

❝ *I am originally from Milan and moved to Rome six years ago to plunge into the world of production.*❞

🍴 Favorite Restaurant
— *Taverna Trilussa*

Via del Politeama, 23-25

This restaurant has both an indoor and outdoor area for seating, and for smokers, a small dedicated area outdoors. Even on colder nights you can still eat out thanks to their outdoor heating. My favorite dish at Trilussa is either a tasty Florentine T-bone steak or anything they do with fish. The service here sets the standard, and the wine is simply perfect.

What do you like most about living in Rome?

❝ *I have a degree in aesthetics, so I appreciate beauty. Everywhere you go, everything you see in this city is dripping beauty. From the humblest fountain to the most elaborate church. Having said that, living in Rome is not that easy, and calls for a lot of patience and thick skin.*❞

Secret Spot
— *Dunes
of Castel
Porziano*

Made or Born Roman?

> *I was born in Rome and have lived here my entire life. I am as Roman as Roman can get, and then some.*

Secret Spot
— *Dunes of Castel Porziano*

I escape there to read a book and breathe the air of the sea. To get there, you have to hike through dense Mediterranean foilage. You pass by stunning archological sites of ancient Roman villas, also once-upon-a-time frequented by celebrities and people of influence seeking the very same things: relaxation and a spiritual retreat.

🍷 Favorite Bar
— *Caffetteria-Bistrot Chiostro del Bramante*

Via Arco della Pace, 5

This is my bar of choice when I want some peace. I typically order a *Marochino* coffee. This is a unique, intimate, and of course historic joint. When I go there, I also gorge on the high renaissance architecture of Donato Bramante, located right across from the bar. It gets pretty busy there, especially before and after events.

> My secret to happiness:
>
> *"Traveling and discovering the world"*

Emanuele

Barista

— *Born and bred in Rome, recommends...*

What do you like most about living in Rome?

> *The beauty, climate, the color of the light, and the history in the air, free to breathe. Rome nurtures my historic roots and ties to it. It's is more than just a city, but an empire, an architectural marvel, and a proud people.*

🍴 Favorite Restaurant
— *Trattoria Romana i Ciarli*

Via Torcegno, 108

I dine at this trattoria every few months. I love the warm atmoshphere, the traditional Roman cuisine, the simplicity and authenticity of the food. Order anything with the tradiational *la contadina* tomatoe sauce, and you will not be disappointed with the freshness of the ingredients, the flavors, and the colors. I usually go there with friends and everyone enjoys it. It has been taken over by a famous Roman chef, which only adds to its unique flavor.

My secret to happiness:
"To be here now"

Marco Pancrazi

Actor

— *Born and bred in Rome, recommends...*

Favorite Spot
— *The stadium of the Foro Italico*

I studied for five years at a vocational university attached to the Foro Italico, dedicated to sports and movement sciences. There is an incredible energy in the air that cannot be described until you walk through the stadium. My best friendships, my most intense memories are all connected to this place.

Favorite Bar
— *Pompi*

Via Albalonga, 7

Without doubt, this place lives up to its claim of being the king of tiramisù. This is a local institution in the San Giovanni neighborhood of Rome. After a long night out, my friends and I always stop for an espresso, or a cold *macchiato freddo* and a tiramisù with shaved chocolate. Simply divine.

Made or Born Roman?

" *I was born in Tivoli, on the outskirts of Rome. Age fourteen onwards, I spent more time in the city training to be an actor and auditioning for roles. Rome raised me in every sense of the word."*

 Favorite Restaurant
— *Bisteak*

Via di Pietralata, 141

This is not a fancy restaurant but more of a trattoria. Still, I have yet to find better quality or more tender meat elsewhere. You choose your cut of meat at the counter, and they cook it to your liking, perfectly. Every time, all the time. The atmosphere is very casual. This is one of those 'must-try' restaurants of the capital.

What do you like most about living in Rome?

" *What I love most about Rome is that it almost feels like a city within a city. When you walk through the streets, even the modern quarters, just turn a corner and you* will find something exquisite, like the Fori Imperiali or a monument that has been a witness to timeless history. It's almost surreal."*

Made or Born Roman?

> **Made.** It was my dream to live in Rome. My husband and I sold everything eight years ago and moved here to start a business and to write."

What do you like most about living in Rome?

> **It keeps me appreciating** the little things in life. Living in an open-air museum, surrounded by history everywhere, is a constant reminder of how insignificant we are. I walk by the Pantheon or see Roman ruins built into the architecture of a piazza from the renaissance and I realize how short it all is."

My secret to happiness:
"To always be authentic, aware and curious, but not to judge"

Jessica Alexander

Writer

— Born in the USA, now based in Rome, recommends...

 Favorite Spot
— *Gianicolo*

The viewpoint from Gianicolo on a clear day. Anywhere I can see the outline of Rome makes me sigh. Rome's beauty is breathtaking. Between the cupolas, the Roman ruins, and the umbrella pines framed in a backdrop of snowy mountains, there really is no other city like it in the world.

 Favorite Bar
— *Caffetteria-Bistrot Chiostro del Bramante*

Via Arco della Pace, 5

Not far from Piazza Navona, this is a former monastery turned cloister, designed by Donato Bramante. With a church-like façade, enjoy coffee or brunch inside while the golden light streams onto your face through the columns, which, like Rome, is an experience that never gets old.

Favorite Restaurant
— *Il Pagliaccio*

Via dei Banchi Vecchi, 129/a

I have had some incredible culinary experiences there. Go during white truffle season and be prepared for a taste extravaganza. The tasting menu changes, but never disappoints. Just make sure to order a taxi if you have it with the wine-tasting menu as well.

My secret to happiness:

"To appreciate the simple things in life and to daydream"

Roberto Bartoli

Businessman

— Born in Sardinia, now based in Rome, recommends...

Made or Born Roman?

" *I am originally from the island of Sardinia, but now consider myself an adopted Roman.*"

🔒 Secret Spot
— Testaccio

This is one of the oldest neighborhoods in Rome. I've been living here since I arrived. What sets it apart is its relative proximity to the most iconic historical monuments of the city, while at the same time maintaining an organic connection to the more authentic Roman way of life. It's a 'melting pot' of various cultures, united by an underlying bohemian spirit.

🏆 Favorite Bar
— Museo Atelier Canova Tadolini

Via del Babuino, 150/a-b

This is not just my favorite bar, but one of the most unique places I've ever seen. Imagine yourself sipping on a coffee, a cappuccino, or a cocktail surrounded by stunning sculptures. This used to be the famous Italian sculptor Adamo Tadolini's studio in the 1800s.

🍴 Favorite Restaurant
— Casa Coppelle

Piazza delle Coppelle, 49

I am in love with this restaurant's sophisticated and contemporary atmosphere. Dimmed lighting, ceilings with exposed wooden beams, and walls covered with ancient books and paintings attract both locals and the odd tourist every now and then. The cuisine ranges from typical Roman dishes to adapted French favorites as well. Ideal also for a cocktail at their uber retro bar.

What do you like most about living in Rome?

" *Twenty years ago I came to study, and as is quite common with transient souls like me, I was taken hostage by Rome's magic. It's simply sweet, sweet, and sweet. Does it have its unique challenges? Of course, but that also adds to its idiosyncrasy.*"

Favorite Restaurant
— *Casa Coppelle*

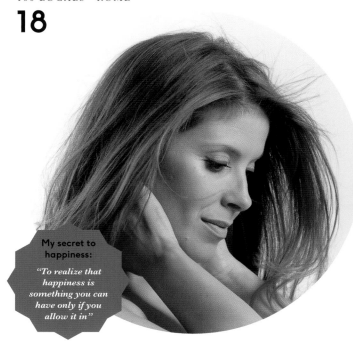

My secret to happiness:

"To realize that happiness is something you can have only if you allow it in"

Mindy Palmer

Full-time Mother

— *Originally from NYC, now based in Rome, recommends...*

Made or Born Roman?

"I moved to Rome from New York after meeting my Roman husband. I've been living here for eight years now."

🔒 Secret Spot
— *Fregene*

This is a small beach town less than half an hour from Rome where the air is clean. It's a great escape from the city, with several beach clubs. My favorite is Ondanomala Suite Club. Perfect for a coffee, lunch, or an *aperitivo*. They have ample seating or you can rent big white lounges that trick you into feeling as if you really *are* on vacation.

🍷 Favorite Bar
— *Il Pozzo del Gelato*

Viale Isacco Newton, 84

My local bar is the most convenient for a coffee. When I have a moment to spare and want to hang out somewhere with exceptional ambience, I go there. The coffee is great and the pastries to die for, which is true of most of the busier bars in the city. But there is something extra special about this one that keeps bringing me back.

🍴 Favorite Restaurant
— *Babette*

Via Margutta, 1D

Located on an old artisans street where *Roman Holiday*, the first American movie filmed entirely in Italy, was shot. The outdoor courtyard is lovely during summertime. The weekend buffet is scrumptious and includes a drink and coffee. Don't miss the *Tortino di Cioccolato Bianco*, a mini cake with a melted white chocolate center.

"The feeling of nostalgia. Knowing that there is so much history that surrounds me at times makes me feel as if I am coasting through a different time. A slower, more relaxed, and simpler time. Knowing that beneath the cobblestones I walk upon lies undiscovered evidence of a life once lived."

What do you like most about living in Rome?

Made or Born Roman?

> *I was born in Denmark. I moved to Rome ten years ago, planning to stay for a year max, but the weather and the food made it impossible to leave.*

Secret Spot
— *Pantheon*

I will always marvel at the many columns and the absolute enormity of the task involved in its construction. I silently chuckle when I imagine the poor workmen questioning Agrippa, the designer, whether two columns rather than three would suffice for this structure.

Favorite Bar
— *Caffetteria-Bistrot Chiostro del Bramante*

I don't drink coffee, but this is where my coffee friends go. Good coffee is integral to Italian life. If you want Romans to respect you, don't ask for tea instead when offered an impromptu coffee. An honorable way out is to say you just had a few double espressos!

Soren Poulsen
Jewelery Company Director

— *Born in Denmark, now based in Rome, recommends...*

What do you like most about living in Rome?

> *The weather and that food is central to life here. The location is fantastic— thirty minutes from the sea, two hours from a major ski resort, and not much further from the hundreds of must-see places across Italy.*

Favorite Restaurant
— *Orazio*

Via Di Porta Latina, 5

My family and I, often with friends, have lunch at this restaurant practically every Sunday. Off the beaten track, fair prices, easy parking, and delicious Roman food. I love the timeless, classic Italian waiters, grumpy at first, but inevitably charming. Try the *Penne alla Vodka* or the succulent lamb dishes grilled on an open fire. The real treat is their massive natural park for you and the kids to run around between meals.

Roman villas
— *Villa Adriana*

🏛 Favorite Restaurant
— *Ai Due Ponti*

Via Flaminia, 858

The name derives from the two bridges where this restaurant is located. A large historic building with an ample garden that is particularly enjoyable after a big meal. This place has fed Rome's socialites and celebrities since time immemorial. There is an incredible buzzing energy permeating the place, which adds to its overall charm.

🍷 Favorite Bar
— *Le Bon Boulanger*

Via Collalto Sabino, 25

Established in 1955, go there for the best coffee in the city. I call them the artists of taste. Delicious aromas the minute you enter. But it's not just the delicious coffees, pastries, and gastronomic delicacies that delight. The warm smiles steal your heart. The baristas have named a drink after me—il misto di Simone—3/4 coffee, 1/4 hot milk.

Made or Born Roman?

" Made. I am an adopted Roman. I moved here in 1997 to study. I fell in love with the city when I first visited in the 1980s."

What do you like most about living in Rome?

" I adore living in Rome simply because it is Roma! I love crossing it from one side to the other to absorb its colors, smells, tastes, culture, ignorance, anger— everything. I am passionate about it be it in daylight or at night. And of course the Romans—their personality, their wealth and poverty, their hypocrisy, their craziness."

My secret to happiness:

"Treat positive things as gifts and the negatives as an opportunity to learn and grow"

Simone Donato

Real Estate Broker

— now based in Rome, recommends...

🍴 Secret Spot
— *Villa Chigi*

This is a marvelous, pristine park in the Trieste neighborhood where I live. It's actually a few locations all in one. I go there to exercise, relax, read, study, or simply to enjoy the first sun rays of spring. It's a great spot for a Sunday picnic and easy to reach. Although it's quite open, you can still find your slice of privacy. For the local residents, this is like our private garden.

Pantheon,
Rome, 2.20 pm

21

My secret to happiness:

"My family, friends, hockey, bicycle, and every passionate pursuit"

Scott Grove

Art Director

—Born in the USA, now based in Rome, recommends...

 ### Secret Spot
— *Pantheon* ⭐

Nothing beats the magic of the Pantheon during a thunder and lightning storm. You have to be lucky to catch the show, but there is nothing more spectacular than gazing at the oculus in the ceiling. You have to hear the acoustics there. Incredible. Sometimes when I am skating through town, I drop by for a quick stroll. Instant rejuvenation.

Favorite Bar
— *Lele and Marta*

Viale Aventino, 57

When I roll up on my skate or bike in the morning, there is always a classic cappuccino being poured just for me. In the afternoons, I never have to say a word, a caffè lungo appears as we discuss the trials and tribulations of everyday Roman life. The entire interaction doesn't take more than two minutes, but it's an important ritual of your day and an integral feature of the DNA of life in this city.

Favorite Restaurant
— *Trattoria dei Cacciatori*

Via Ardeatina, 402

My family and I have been going to eat with Gianni and his boys for years. Gianni is the owner, *maître d'*, and part-time chef. His sons are the waiters, pizza chefs, and grill masters. This is the perfect Italian setting. The food is all hand-crafted, traditional, rustic, and quintessentially Roman. Fantastic pasta dishes, creative pizza toppings, succulent meats on the grill, and out-of-this-world homemade desserts. They know us by name and even on the busiest nights they will squeeze us in. In summer you sit in the outdoor garden, and in the colder months it's nice and cozy inside with the wood-fire grill heating up the dining room.

Made or Born Roman?

Made. I have been in Rome for more than twenty-two years. Came for the adventure and stayed."

What do you love most about Rome?

I love the silent contracts you enter with your local food vendors, the hardware store, your local bars and restaurants. Once you are taken in as part of the family, money is not always needed. Reservations can be overlooked. There is never a stupid question about a new vegetable, fruit, or fish. They will tell you how their mother prepares it, and at times, bring you samples. You can make your mark in Rome if you give Rome the freedom to leave its mark on you. This is the ultimate secret of success here."

Favorite Bar
— *Lele and Marta*

My secret to happiness:

"Dedicating my life to my children, who fill my soul with joy"

Michela Ursini

Architect

— *Born and bred in Rome, recommends...*

Made or Born Roman?

I was born a Roman and have been living here since. No matter where I travel, Rome is where my heart yearns to be."

Secret Spot — *Villa Pamphili*

This is the perfect spot for jogging, relaxing in the wide open air, or for fun picnics with children. My parents reside very close to the park, so when I was still living with them, I used to hang out there often. Although I live elsewhere in Rome now, I still take my kids back there and they love it. It's a perfect spot for personal time and meditation, as well as lively gatherings of friends and loved ones.

Favorite Bar — *Conca d'Oro*

Viale America, 29

Adjacent to the EUR lake and park, this bar has been renovated recently and has a vibrant and modern feel to it. It's also a top-notch pastry shop. Delicious aromas of freshly baked croissants will greet you as soon as you walk in. I take my coffee in a glass with a little sugar, although their blend is very smooth and not at all bitter. Service is fast, friendly, and efficient.

Favorite Restaurant — *Le Mani in Pasta*

Via dei Genovesi, 37

This is my favorite restaurant in the heart of Trastevere. The seafood and the meats are equally superb. Relaxed, casual with warm and attentive staff. Fair prices for the quality of the food. Spadino is the owner and chef and has known my family for years. Try the carpaccio of seabass and truffle, with warm buns and butter. A reservation is a must.

What do you like most about living in Rome?

Rome is the eternal city where the past, the present, and the future merge with endless possibilities. The joy of living here is immense and there is something for everyone. Museums, cycling by the river, a retreat to a green oasis like Villa Borghese or Villa Ada, or even a day out at the Olympic stadium to support your favorite soccer team."

Made or Born Roman?

> *I was born in Catanzaro, in Calabria, and moved to Rome about twenty years ago for university. Like many Calabrians who do just that, I never left.*

What do you like most about living in Rome?

> *The ever-changing landscape of the city. Many times I find myself in a place I know I've been to many times before, but just realize that there behind a corner lies a place unknown waiting to be discovered.*

🍦 Favorite Bar
— *Gelateria Pasticceria Ornelli*

Via Merulana, 232

If you have a sweet tooth, you have to check this place out. It's more than a bar, more than a pastry shop, and more than a gelateria. It's all three put together, each done exceptionally well. Their homemade cakes come in many varieties, and are best enjoyed with a delicious coffee.

🔒 Secret Spot
— *National Museum of Oriental Art*

Housed in one of the most distinguished buildings in the city, this museum holds the collections of Giuseppe Tucci. Art pieces from Tibet, China, and India circa the 1920s and 1930s. Possibly the least visited museum in Rome because I suspect oriental art is a fringe interest in Italy. But this allows you to enjoy and absorb its beauty in tranquility.

Domenico Donato

Lawyer

— *Born and bred in Rome, recommends...*

🍴 Favorite Restaurant
— *Club Machiavelli*

Via Machiavelli, 49

Mauro is the owner and chef. His knowledge of traditional Roman and Italian cuisine is profound. But he adds a modern twist. The atmosphere is very homey, intimate, and cordial. Most evenings there, and wind down with Mauro at our table, entertaining us with his culinary adventures and the back stories of the dishes we just ate. The place is not very big, which means you don't have to raise your voice to be heard.

Favorite
Restaurant
— *Pizzeria
Antica Stabia*

Made or Born Roman?

> *I was born in Rome, raised in Rome, and I cannot imagine myself living anywhere else but Rome."*

🔒 Secret Spot
— *Campidoglio*

If you are like me and enjoy tucked-away locations, I bet you will fall in love with this very secluded corner, right behind the Campidoglio, one of the seven hills of Rome. You will never find many people there, which adds to its romantic allure. No sooner do you get there, than you feel you've been literally catapulted back in time, with Roman ruins at your feet, illuminated at night as if it were a theatre. A perfect spot for a special toast.

🍷 Favorite Bar ⭐
— *Bar del Fico*

Piazza del Fico, 26

My favorite drink there is a decadent coffee called *il Marocchino*—served in a small glass with a dash of chocolate, a generous sprinkle of bitter cocoa, and an optional topping of cream. The inside of this place is shabby chic and many have tried but failed to imitate it. One of those rare bars that's alive in the mornings and through the wee hours of the night when rambunctious Romans take over.

My secret to happiness:
"To be positive, especially when life makes it impossible to be so"

Martina Della Corte

Physician

— Born and bred in Rome, recommends...

What do you like most about living in Rome?

> *Rome offers everyone a taste of everything. Where to go, what to eat, even when to eat. Depending on your mood, you can always find the right spot for that moment. Now imagine all that coupled with the most amazing weather one can ask for. I rest my case!"*

🍴 Favorite Restaurant
— *Pizzeria Antica Stabia*

Via Tiburtina, 613

I go there to get my favorite pizza in town prepared by Don Raffaele, who is also the owner. As he prepares your pizza, he enjoys watching you and guessing small secrets about your life. You can play along if you want. Crystal-ball skills aside, his pizzas are bursting with flavor and homegrown produce. When you're done and are ready to leave, Don Raffaele never lets you leave empty-handed. The last time I walked out with a freshly baked loaf of bread.

My secret to happiness:

"To be self-contented and surrounded by true friends"

Simone Tafoni

Sales Agent

— *Born in Santa Severa, now based in Rome, recommends...*

— *Chiesa Nuova*

When I am in need of a break from the world and all its chaos, I find solace in the beautiful churches of this city. One of my favorites is Santa Maria in Vallicella, also known as the Chiesa Nuova. It is the principal church of the Oratorians, a religious congregation of secular priests. Even if you are not religious, churches impart a sense of serenity when you visit.

— *Bar L'Archetto*

Via dell'Archetto, 26

This is one of my all-time favorite bars, super close to the Tiber. Visit a few times and they will start calling you by name and remembering exactly how you like your coffee. Try the 'Roman muffin' with a freshly squeezed orange juice.

Made or Born Roman?

> *I am from a town just outside Rome by the sea called Santa Severa, but I transferred to Rome eight years ago."*

What do you like most about living in Rome?

> *This city is alive all year round. It has a certain unique charm and glamour that imparts a new flavor to life every day. I come from a very small town where art and culture are limited, so I appreciate the abundance here."*

Favorite Restaurant
— *Osteria Pucci*

Piazza Mastai, 1

A bit on the expensive side, but every now and then when I want to pamper myself, I go there. If you are a soup lover, this is the place to try, especially on a cold winter day. The flavors are very delicate and unique, and the service is impeccable. On weekends and holidays, it may be prudent to make a reservation.

Made or Born Roman?

> *I was born in Rome, but have also lived elsewhere due to the nature of my job. Nothing beats Rome though. There is a very good reason they call it the eternal city. Nothing beats the sense of eternity of Rome."*

Secret Spot
— *Colosseum*

Ever since I was a kid, I was attracted to this iconic Roman monument, which encapsulates the essence of the city. I face it and am in awe of how just 2,000 years ago, people, aristocracy, and the clergy coexisted. It's the happy and colorful slice of the city—insane during the day, but enveloped by a wave of serenity in the evening. Sipping a cocktail or a simple beer facing the Colosseum is always priceless.

Favorite Bar
— *Garden Bar*

Via Livorno, 11

By definition, all Roman bars make you feel at home. But this place is my absolute favorite. It's right across from my office, and is as Roman of a bar as you can get. You'll see everyone here. A rich tapestry of a vibrant city. All I have to do is walk in and the barista starts preparing my *latte macchiato con cacao* (hot milk with a dash of coffee and a sprinkle of cocoa powder), and in the morning, my favorite croissant.

My secret to happiness:

"Don't take yourself too seriously, and laugh or you will age quicker"

Diego Cannella

Army Officer

— *Born and bred in Rome, recommends...*

What do you like most about living in Rome?

> *Going through the historic center feels like you're traveling through time. Roads named after flowers, ancient citizens, queens, and emperors. To be able to balance the chaotic rhythm of the city with its tranquility renders the entire experience of being Roman incredible."*

Favorite Restaurant
— *Taverna Lucifero*

Via dei Cappellari, 28

This place strikes the perfect balance of quality food, affordable prices, an authentic Roman kitchen, and off-the-beaten track. This is where real Romans come out to dine. It's not just the mouth-watering food but the overall experience that leaves me feeling at peace, and in sync with the city. The presentation of the dishes is impeccable and the portions are very generous. Do not miss the goose breast with truffles (*il petto d'oca al tartufo*). You'll come back for that, I guarantee it.

My secret to happiness:

"A family to be proud of, lots of sports, a rewarding job, and great food"

Andrea Taiani

Tax Inspector

— A Roman convert, recommends...

Favorite Restaurant
— Pane Vino e San Daniele

Piazza Mattei, 16

This centrally located restaurant is tucked deep inside the Jewish ghetto, which means it's easily accessible but still by-and-large off the tourist radar. If you do dine there, make an expedition out of it to discover this fascinating part of the city. The menu is simple, but offers original options for finicky eaters. The wild boar is a must, as is anything they do with truffles. The wine selection is smartly matched to the food. All of this is topped by excellent service and fair prices.

Made or Born Roman?

> *I moved to Rome in 2007 for work, so a Roman convert. The city has this amazing magnetic power to transform everyone in its image. I cannot think of anywhere else I would like to live now.*

What do you like most about living in Rome?

> *No city in the world is really able to transmit such a strong sense of history and identity at each and every corner, and to balance that perfectly with the quintessentially chaotic nature of its citizens. It is this uniqueness that draws people to the city and makes its longtime residents proud of their roots.*

Favorite Bar
— Bar Bistrot Gusto Massimo

Via del Circo Massimo, 5

This is my second home. They greet me by name and my drink is usually ready at the counter by the time I get there. Their coffees is to die for and their selection of wines, beers, and prosecco for evening aperitifs is excellent. Enjoy your drink overlooking the Circo Massimo with the Fori Imperiali as your backdrop. It doesn't get much better than this.

Secret Spot
— Altare della Patria

This monument was built in honor of Victor Emmanuel, the first king of a unified Italy. A unique, historical symbol of power that has witnessed the golden years of this country's glory. For years it has been the stage of important national events accentuating its significance. On it you will find the key values engraved in the marble—the unity of the country and the freedom of its citizens.

My secret to happiness:

"Take what the world has given me as a gift"

Fiorella

Marketing and Communication Expert

— *Born and bred in Rome, recommends...*

Made or Born Roman?

" *Rome is a magnet for many immigrants, both from within Italy and across the world, but I am a proud Roman by birth.*"

🔒 Secret Spot
— *Piazza Navona*

I work in the heart of the city. From my window, I glimpse Piazza Navona. Its touristic allure aside, it's a place that charms at all hours and seasons. In summer, during the early hours of the morning, enjoy the deserted atmosphere when you will not hear a squeak. Then in winter, the evenings are cozy with the warmly decorated restaurants circling the square and the roasted chestnut vendors.

🍷 Favorite Bar
— *I Dolci di Nonna Vincenza*

Via dell'Arco del Monte, 98

I try to exercise restraint with pastries and cakes, but this bar is where I fail miserably. Everything they craft, they do with love. When I walk in, every piece of cake calls out my name. Most of the pastries they make are Sicilian. This being Rome, the coffees are outstanding and the ambience complements the whole experience.

🍴 Favorite Restaurant
— *Osteria Scaloni*

Via Carlo Mirabello, 8A

I have grown to be quite loyal to this place. Everything about it is delightful, including the cordial service and the refined menu. The specials change every day depending on what is in season. One of their unique dishes, which I highly recommend, is testarolo. This is made from a traditional pasta that is almost impossible to find in Rome.

What do you like most about living in Rome?

" *The city always surprises me. Does it have its frustrations and challenges? Sure, like most big cities.*
But I could never live elsewhere. Rome is like a difficult lover. She challenges you, but her beauty always prevails."

Favorite Bar
— *Sant'Eustachio Il Caffè*

Piazza di Sant'Eustachio, 82

This bar is located right across from the Senate, but I would say its real claim to fame has to be that it serves the best coffee in town. I could start describing it, but I'd rob you of the experience. Just go there and grab a grancaffé, then thank me.

Made or Born Roman?

I was born in Rome but lived overseas for a few years. As much as I like to travel to discover the world, Rome is my eternal home."

What do you like most about living in Rome?

The best thing about this city is that it allows you to live it in many ways. You can lose yourself in the stunning historical tapestry, or if you love the outdoors, you can enjoy the city's endless swathes of greenery. Rome can be as big or small as you make of it."

My secret to happiness:
"To never stop being a dreamer"

Minou Mebane

Psychologist

— *Born and bred in Rome, recommends...*

Secret Spot
— *Gianicolo Hill*

This is my absolute favorite spot in the city. Although not one of the famous Seven Hills of Rome, it offers what I believe is the most exquisite panoramic view of the city. This is a wonderful sanctuary to relax and re-energize. Oftentimes I find myself gravitating there for no particular reason. Gazing out and meditating has the amazing power to heal my life.

Favorite Restaurant
— *Sor'Eva*

Piazza della Rovere, 108

I've been eating here for as long as I hold memories. Originally a wine cellar named after its very first owner, Eva, it's been in business as a restaurant since 1937. There you can feast on typical Roman fare at reasonable prices. Their pizzas are also not to be missed. In the fifties and sixties this was the 'it' place for after-hours gatherings of theater glitterati.

Favorite Bar
— *Bar Pasticceria Riccomi*

Made or Born Roman?

> *I moved to Rome in 1999 for work, despite the fact that I could have easily worked closer to my hometown, but Rome always attracted me. And that was a good move because I met my future husband there.*

> *Rome is home. Its eternal beauty embraces me. As a city, it is as good as it gets in terms of art, history, culture, theaters, restaurants, and entertainment for children. I love the myriad green areas you find around old Roman villas. Even as a busy professional, the rare times I am able to escape for a reprieve makes it all worth it. I dive into its beauty and fall in love with Rome all over again!*

What do you like most about living in Rome?

My secret to happiness:
"To keep work and home separate"

 ## Favorite Restaurant
— Il Tempio di Iside

Via Labicana, 50

Look out for Francesco, the owner who sometimes waits the tables. A wonderful man. Seafood is the specialty here. Raw or cooked, it's always deliciously prepared and served with a touch of elegance that will leave you speechless. Start with a *crostino con mazzancolla* (toasted bread with prawns) and *lardo di colonnata* (*salumi* made by curing strips of fatback) drizzled with balsamic vinegar, then work your way to *la burrata* cheese served with anchovies or a catalana of shrimps and scampi. Their homemade fruit ice cream crowns it all.

Serena Triboldi

Lawyer

— *Based in Rome, recommends...*

 ## Secret Spot
— Orto botanico in Trastevere

Trastevere is easily one of the most vibrant spots, but amidst the chaos you will be pleasantly surprised to find this oasis called the orto botanico. When I was a law student many years ago, I used to escape there to study or clear my mind. Now I take my kids to explore nature away from the hustle and bustle of the city.

 ## Favorite Bar
— Bar Pasticceria Riccomi

Via Gregorio VII, 54

I am not much of a coffee drinker compared to the rest of my compatriots, but if I were, I don't think I'd go anywhere other than this place. But I still go there for the pastries, and their wholemeal croissant with honey, served soft and warm, is as good as it gets.

My secret to happiness:

"To appreciate what life has generously given me without taking it for granted"

Olivier Christophe

Marketing Manager

— Adopted by Rome, recommends...

🔒 Secret Spot
— *Garbatella*

This lesser-known part of Rome is often overlooked. The architecture is unique and in perfect harmony with the picturesque surroundings. Very different from central Rome. Balconies and terraces brimming with character, symmetrical gardens, and lazy gatherings of the elderly sharing neighborhood gossip. I feel time simply stopped moving in this charming part of Rome. For soccer lovers, know that Garbatella is a stronghold of Roma fans!

🏆 Favorite Bar
— *Bar Tornatora*

Via Oderisi da Gubbio, 27-29

The popularity of this bar is evident by the amount of croissant crumbs you will find every morning on the floor, the real color of which is probably unknown. Their pastries are prepared with love, and like most bars in this city, they take their coffee very seriously. This would be as good as any spot to see authentic Romans in their natural element.

Made or Born Roman?

> *My desire for adventure and my sweet tooth for Italian cuisine brought me to Rome in 1997. I have been a proud adopted Roman ever since."*

🍴 Favorite Restaurant
— *Trattoria Cadorna*

Via Raffaele Cadorna, 12

A family-run business, where the mother cooks, the father sources the produce, and the kids wait and manage the restaurant. These are the ideal ingredients of the perfect restaurant. My meal always starts with the Cadorna Appetizer, which includes *melanzane con mozzarella di bufala* (eggplants topped with melted buffalo mozazarella cheese).

What do you like most about living in Rome?

> *The most romantic and colorful sunsets, the beauty of the city, the classical monuments all around the city, the rich history, the chaos, and last but definitely not least, the beauty of Roman women."*

Loving Rome
— *Romantic views*

My secret to happiness:

"To accept that pain and sadness are also part of life"

Rosa Capuana

Analyst

— *Born in Naples, based in Rome, recommends...*

Made or Born Roman?

 I am an adopted Roman. Like many before me, and many after me, I migrated north from Napoli in 2003 for work, and never went back."

🔓 Secret Spot
— *Piazza Farnese*

I am in love with almost every piazza in this city, but the one that allows me to fully detach from my world is Piazza Farnese with its nuanced beauty and elegant surrounding buildings. I keep it simple and usually sit on one of the sides of this square to observe the majestic buildings that bound it. Invariably, this leaves me speechless.

🏆 Favorite Bar
— *Bar Caffetteria Pasquino*

Via del Governo Vecchio, 79

I'll whisper this because I fear my citizenship may be stripped after this revelation, but I am not a coffee lover. However, mix it with milk, and I am more amenable to it. My coffee credentials aside, I know from experience that if you are a coffee maven, this is as good as it gets. Their beverages are highly original, as is their presentation.

🍴 Favorite Restaurant
— *L'Archetto*

Via dell' Archetto, 26

When I have friends visiting, my first instinct is to take them to this place to show off the very best of Italian cuisine. There are many renditions and varieties of the quintessentially Roman pasta, the famous carbonara, but you would be hard-pressed to find a place that whips it up better.

What do you like most about living in Rome?

Rome is not shy about exposing its beauty in every season. Let's face it, the winters are not harsh by any standard, while spring and summer bloom with life, color, and a cornocopia of exciting new places to see and explore. I think of Rome as a factory of the most memorable experiences one can have."

Made or Born Roman?

> *One hundred percent Roman, born and raised. I have, however, lived abroad most of my life and finally returned to Rome two years ago.*

🔒 Secret Spot
— *Villa Borghese*

The bond between nature, history, and the city is incredible there. You are at the very heart of the city and yet you are immersed in nature, surrounded by green, encased by the most peaceful silence. And the city is watching your every step and feeling, reminding you how beautiful it is, by peeking at you from its historical tops visible between the glorious trees. Sip a coffee at one of the many scattered bars, read on a bench, or rent a bike or a Segway.

🍷 Favorite Bar
— *Il Naturista*

Via dei Georgofili, 44

This tiny, unassuming neighborhood bar exemplifies the authentic Rome many tourists may never see. The owners are a lovely couple who cook heavenly fare— homemade lasagna, delicious pies, and divine cakes. Like me, most customers are regulars who keep an open tab. Best of all, you will always find the requisite elderly couple sitting outside basking in the sun like cats.

My secret to happiness: *"Understanding that there aren't any universal truths"*

Giulia La Rosa

Business Owner

— Born and bred in Rome, recommends...

What do you like most about living in Rome?

> *The weather above all. Also its proximity to the beach, the countryside, the mountains, and the many lakes nearby. Despite its fast pace, Rome is always a welcoming place and you will always find someone eager to listen and visualize the bigger picture with you if you have the time.*

🍴 Favorite Restaurant
— *Perilli*

Via Marmorata, 39

There are many restaurants in Rome to match the many moods the city inspires on any given day. One of my favorites happens to also be one of the oldest restaurants in the Testaccio neighborhood. They uphold an incredible family tradition of *guanciale* (cheek lard) aging. The result is one of the best carbonara pastas you will ever have. This is a small, typical Roman trattoria with a convivial, jolly atmosphere.

Loving Rome
— *A city wide awake*

🔒 Secret Spot
— *Colle Oppio*

There is an infinite number of magnificent spots of eternal beauty in Rome, but Colle Oppio is my favorite. This is the southern spur of the Esquiline Hill, one of the famous Seven Hills of Rome. It offers an unparalleled view of the majestic Colosseum. I go there to observe and marvel, and to connect the gaps between past, present, and future. I always get entangled in strong feelings of gratitude to be living amongst all these cultural treasures.

🍷 Favorite Bar
— *Bar Trecastelli*

Via dei Georgofili, 91

This is my local bar, a proud staple of our neighborhood since 1978. Sometimes people get attached to their local bar for convenience. In my case, I love this place regardless of its proximity, but for the standard of its service and quality of its coffees and pastries. No matter what the weather is like, it's always warm there. Even before I make my way to the counter, my cappuccino is ready with a sweet shape of a heart adorning the foam.

My secret to happiness:

"Having something to do, something to believe in, and someone to love"

Monica Ferreccio

Team Leader

— *Born and bred in Rome, recommends...*

Made or Born Roman?

What do you like most about living in Rome?

❝ *With the exception of longer overseas trips, I have been living in Rome ever since I was born.*❞

❝ *Probably the best weather one can ask for with mild seasons. The comforting smell of home after long spells of rain. The vibrant sounds of cars and people that animate the city. The vast options of where to shop, dine, and have fun, keeping the city wide awake. All these things affect my life positively.*❞

Favorite Restaurant
— *Dal Sorcetto*

Via Civitavecchia, 24, Rome

Don't let the name of this restaurant turn you off. Sorcetto is a typical Roman expression for a rat. Semantics and odd names apart, this is a gem of a restaurant where real Romans dine. A terrific location, perfect ambience, with friendly and extremely efficient service. Seafood lovers and carnivores coexist happily here where magic with truffles and mushrooms transpires. Their homemade pastas will leave you pondering 'what just happened' for a long time after.

My secret to happiness:

"To appreciate what I have while allowing myself to dream of what I don't"

Ellery
Lawyer

— *Born and bred in Rome, recommends...*

Favorite Restaurant
— *Dar Filettaro a Santa Barbara*

Largo dei Librari, 88

This place is more than just a restaurant offering typically Roman fare. It serves only a few dishes but it does them exceptionally well, which has propelled it to a cult status. My favorite dish there is the fried codfish, with a few of their original side dishes that are impossible to find elsewhere. The internal atmosphere is quite sparse, which is compensated for by the surroundings, including the ancient baroque church of Santa Barbara.

Made or Born Roman?

Roman by birth, although recently I've been spending substantial periods of time in Naples for work. Still, when I get back to Rome it always feels like my eternal home."

 Secret Spot
— *Corsini Botanical Gardens*

One of Rome's unique features are its numerous public parks and gardens, open to everyone to explore and to enjoy for a jog, a stroll, or simply to lie down and steal a moment of relaxation. The historical Palazzo Corsini of the Corsini gardens is part of the Orto Botanico di Roma, a botanical garden operated by the Sapienza University of Rome.

Favorite Bar
— *Antica Latteria*

Vicolo del Gallo, 8

I used to think of bars as transient stops for a very quick coffee until I discovered this place. I make it a point to choose a strategic spot where I can sip my warm chocolate while enjoying the rich surroundings. There, time seems to be on pause, even for the owner, whose mannerisms may not be considered appropriate by today's standards, but still charming.

What do you like most about living in Rome?

Rome, despite its numerous flaws in terms of public transport and manageability, still holds the title of caput mundi. Whatever negativity we are confronted with, we are compensated amply by our surroundings, which never cease to surprise us. Few cities can be this dynamic."

Made or Born Roman?

> *I moved to Rome for work and fell in love with an Italian and never left.*"

Secret Spot
— *Piazza di Pietra*

This is a jewel in the heart of the city. The name of the square refers to the grandiose stone columns of a temple to Emperor Hadrian built in 144 AD by his successor, Antoninus Pius. Whenever I have a need to decompress, and to step aside from the day-to-day inanities, I take refuge there. The scale of the columns and the history engraved in it put life in perspective.

Favorite Bar
— *Caffè Perù*

Via di Monserrato, 46

Piazza Farnese, where I work, is riddled with many-a-bars. But hands down this is my favorite one. Their coffee is somehow more intense, more robust, and always comes with a mini-dark chocolate on the side that you can eat or keep for later. I come here for caffeine on the run or for longer, lazier respites.

My secret to happiness:
"I don't have one, but if one exists, I am pretty sure you can find it in Rome!"

Salina Grenet
Diplomat

— *Born in France, heart stolen by a Roman, recommends...*

What do you like most about living in Rome?

> *I could not imagine myself living anywhere but Rome. Still, to survive here you have to be tenacious. Whatever the downside is, it's more than made up for by the architecture, culinary adventures, breathtaking colors, the weather, and how every road here tells a story.*"

Favorite Restaurant
— *Vineria il Chianti*

Via del Lavatore, 81

Common sense dictates that you stay away from restaurants close to the main touristic sites. This joint, however, defies that rule. Don't hold its proximity to Fontana di Trevi against it. It has all the ingredients to make you fall in love with it. Excellent, efficient, and well-mannered staff and phenomenal food.

My secret to happiness:

"Not to take anything for granted and to keep the kid inside of me always alive"

Carolina Cenci

Advertising Executive

— Born and based in Rome, recommends...

 I was born in Rome but was raised in the outskirts in an area known as the Castelli Romani noted for its particular dishes, wine, and landscape."

Secret Spot
— *Il Buco*

Whenever I have friends visiting from abroad I always take them to this place because secretly I want to experience it over and over again. This is essentially an incredible view through a little tiny hole found on the entrance gate of an important building of the Knights of Malta. I could tell you exactly how to get there but that would ruin half the fun.

Favorite Bar
— *Zerozero100*

Via del Verano, 27

It's not simply a morning bar, but rather an-every-moment bar! I usually stop by for a drink after work—it's my personal time to wind down. I always love to chat with the owners and the other regular customers and exchange some gossip and jokes before heading back home. And yes, their coffee is really great too.

Favorite Restaurant
— *L'Osteria di Monteverde*

Via Pietro Cartoni, 163

One day three best friends who were tired of their menial jobs decided to enrich this friendship by teaming up and launching what has become one of the most successful restaurants in the area of Monteverde. Their charisma, coupled with their passion for food and wine, makes this one of my favorite eateries. Their menu is always understated, a feature I love. Every time I go, I try something new, and I am never disappointed.

What do you like most about living in Rome?

I am fascinated by how the sun reflects off Roman monuments. I cannot live without the air I breathe when I take a stroll around the tiny roads in the heart of the city. It feels like home. When I leave for a holiday, no matter how long or short, I always yearn for Rome at some level, but especially the unique Roman sense of humor and irony."

My secret to happiness:

"To see the glass half full"

Lucrezia Villalta

Media Professional

— *Born and bred in Rome, recommends...*

 Favorite Restaurant
— *Osteria da Francesco*

Via Valsugana, 48/52, Roma

Due to the nature of my job, I have tested and reviewed thousands of restaurants in town. My favorite by far is the Osteria da Francesco. Named after the owner, who is pretty much a fixture of the place, always cheerful as he greets his customers and makes them feel at home. He is constantly adapting his menu to delight his regulars with new creations and classic homemade dishes. I usually never need a menu. I trust him to feed me what he thinks is best on that day.

Made or Born Roman?

 I was born and raised in 'la mia Roma!"

Secret Spot
— *Belvedere*

When I am in need of some time off from the world, I usually go down to the 'Belvedere' on the Gianicolo. For the past ten years, if not more, I still sit on the same marble bench, which has a first-class view of my favorite, most beautiful city. As I watch the world go by, I unwind and am filled with gratitude that what I am looking at is where I live.

Favorite Bar
— *Ciampini*

Piazza San Lorenzo in Lucina, 29

The sun always shines on this square at any time of the day, whether I go for a quick cappuccino in the morning or for an afternoon drink with my friends. I never forget to include in my order the small round mini-pizza prepared fresh on the hour. The cherry on the top in this bar is the *granita al caffè con panna*, or crunched iced coffee with cream.

What do you like most about living in Rome?

 Rome is a city for all people at all times. Amazing food, the hottest fashions, culture coming out of its ears, even sports and outdoor activities—it's got it all. Not to mention that we're close to both the beach and the mountains. And no other city beats Rome's weather!"

Made or Born Roman?

66 *I was born in Rome fifty-six years ago and have neither lived anywhere else nor do I want to."*

What do you like most about living in Rome?

66 *I am not a well-heeled traveler, but I know what foreigners love when they visit my city. It's the weather, the Roman sense of humor, and the incredible stories told by the abounding monuments. If you close your eyes and imagine you are a gladiator, you may just believe it."*

🔒 Secret Spot
— *Villa Medici Del Vascello*

This villa is a picturesque amalgamation of a military structure and a suburban Roman villa, built in the early fifteenth century. It's breathtaking in every possible way, surrounded by manicured gardens and evocative sculptures. I go there to meditate spiritually, but it's also a fun day out for a family with kids.

🍷 Favorite Bar
— *Bar Trecastelli*

Via dei Georgofili, 91

The Neapolitans have a famous saying, *cavolo, come coce,* or *damn, this is good,* and that's what this bar invokes in most people. Now in the interest of full disclosure, I am one of the proprietors of this place, but I challenge you to try our coffees or pastries and still feel I am biased. If you come by, ask for me and come say hello!

My secret to happiness:

"To be self-deprecating, merciful, and love others unconditionally..."

Maurizio Palescandolo

Entrepreneur

— Born and bred in Rome, recommends...

🍴 Favorite Restaurant
— *Il Gabriello*

Via Vittoria, 51

This place is a quick stroll from what is possibly the most beautiful and magical square in Rome, Piazza di Spagna. Given the popularity of the location, it is remarkable how this place remains authentic. The specialty there is *riso con la crema di scampi* (risotto with the cream of scampi). I'll guarantee you two things when you leave this place—a full stomach and an extremely satisfied temperament.

Favorite Bar
— *Ciampini*

Made or Born Roman?

" *I hail from Neapolitan roots, but was born near Rome, in the seaside town of Ostia. I consider myself one hundred percent Roman.*"

My secret to happiness:

"To never expect too much from the future and to focus on the present"

🔒 Secret Spot
— *Villa Borghese*

This is my all-time favorite spot in Rome. I am particularly in love with the gardens, which are very close to the zoo. Whether you want to take a romantic walk with a loved one or if you enjoy a full workout surrounded by nature and historical monuments, I can't think of a better place to do either. The atmosphere is simply magical. You can also rent bikes there.

💡 Favorite Bar
— *Ciampini*

Piazza di S. Lorenzo in Lucina, 29

In one of the hippest neighborhoods of Rome, this bar is frequented mostly by young adults and students. I can confidently claim their gelato is the best in town. Their coffee stands out, whether you take it as an espresso or with milk, like a cappuccino or *caffè latte*. You can enjoy all of this while perched outside facing the picturesque square.

Noemi Smorra

Singer/Actress

— *Neapolitan roots, now based in Rome, recommends...*

What do you like most about living in Rome?

" *Living in Rome is like a love story. Try as I might, frankly, I cannot imagine myself living anywhere else. The beauty of the city is the sort that leaves you speechless. Even when you are stuck in traffic, just gaze out at the diverse scenery, monuments, and the ever-present sense of incredible history and it will all be worth it.*"

Favorite Restaurant
— *Da Cocco*

Via Circonvallazione Appia, 37

Despite my Napolitan origins, where the pizza tends to be quite thick, I prefer the crunchy, thinner pizzas that are more common in Rome. This joint is my hot recommendation for the best Roman-style pizza you can get in this town. Trust me on this—the pizzas are baked in a wood-fire oven built in 1936. The atmosphere is cozy and the furniture retro, which adds plenty of character. Not to be missed if you are a pizza-head like myself.

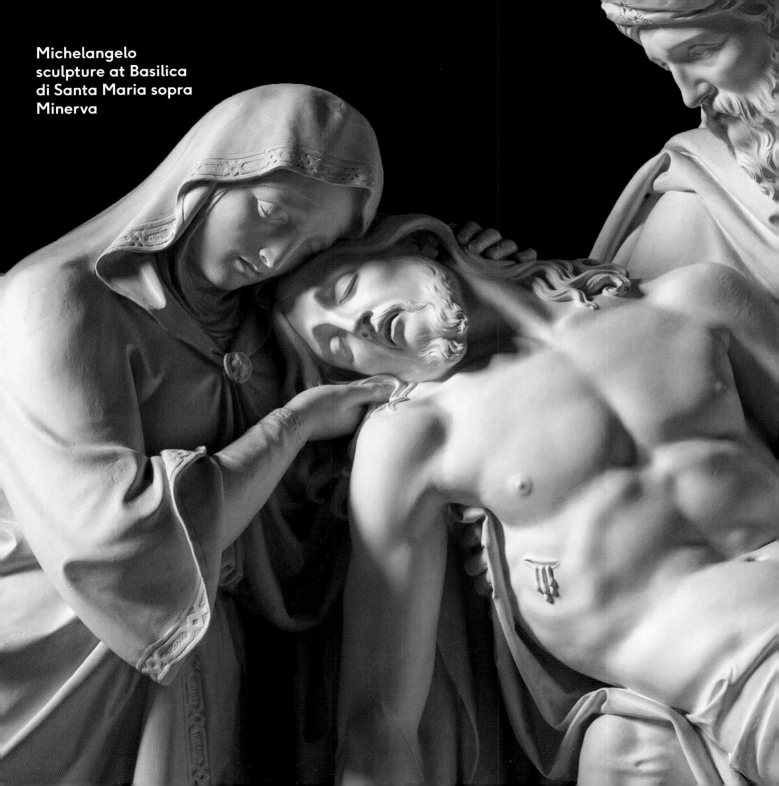

Michelangelo sculpture at Basilica di Santa Maria sopra Minerva

41

My secret to happiness:

"Good music, good food, and a good glass of red wine"

Daniele Papa

Advertising Exectutive

— *Born in Umbria, now based in Rome, recommends...*

What do you like most about living in Rome?

> *Rome offers everything, but you have to know your way around it and never allow it to conquer you. I can't deny there are numerous logistical problems associated with living here, but when I do the math, the positive far outweighs anything else."*

🔒 Secret Spot
— *Monteverde*

Some like to walk between the tiny roads in the center of the city, but my secret spot preference is actually an area, not known to those living north of Rome, called Monteverde. Its most attractive feature is that it is perched on a hill that overlooks the entire city. On the worst of days, the view will leave you lost for words, which for many Romans is a biological impossibility.

🏆 Favorite Bar
— *The Barkings*

Via Appia Nuova, 457

When I step in this bar I always hear "Buongiorno Daniele!" and there's no better way to start my day. Their breakfast *cornetto*s are to die for. I try to resist each time, but I fail. My greatest indulgence are their mini corenttos filled with homemade cream. With the perfect coffee to match, I leave the bar ready for my Roman day!

🍴 Favorite Restaurant
— *Trattoria Epiro*

Piazza Epiro, 25

Not everything good has to be historic. This newly opened bistro has a youthful staff who are eager to pamper you and make sure you don't leave with a micron of empty space in your belly. As it is not very touristic, the ratio of quality to price is superb, with a rich selection of wine.

Made or Born Roman?

> *I moved to Rome about ten years ago from the Umbria region looking for interesting job opportunities, and, as you would expect, I have yet to move back!"*

My secret to happiness:

"Figuring out how to improve myself and evolve..."

Emanuele di Marco

Photographer

— *Born and bred in Rome, recommends...*

Made or Born Roman?

I was born in Frascati on the outskirts of Rome, but moved to the city soon after. While I have ties to Frascati, Rome is where my heart is rooted now."

Secret Spot
— *Giardino degli Aranci*

This is my most visited little secret haven. It's a cozy place surrounded by plenty of lush greenery. It's the ideal place to visit in the late afternoon. I usually go there when I am seeking peace and quiet away from all the traffic, chaos, and noise of the city streets.

Favorite Bar
— *Antico Caffè Greco*

Via dei Condotti, 86

This bar is not too far from the Pantheon. In addition to delicious coffee, their speciality is the *granita di caffè*, or crushed-ice coffee. This is a must-try Roman staple, and no place does it better than this institution of a bar. Perfect to hang out in both during warm and cool days.

Favorite Restaurant
— *Checco er Carettiere*

Via Benedetta, 10

This is a historic joint run by three generations of the same family. It depicts perfectly the true vibe of the neighborhood, also known as *la Roma Trasteverina*. When my friends and I decide to eat at *da Checco*, suddenly we're all smiles from ear to ear, looking forward to an outstanding meal.

What do you like most about living in Rome?

I love how you will always find someone who appreciates this city, despite its many flaws. Living in Rome is not easy, especially considering traffic and pollution. So when you meet people who abstain from judging her, and love her for what she stands for, you suddenly see and live the city under a totally new light."

Made or Born Roman?

> *I have been living in Rome for nineteen years. I moved here from Puglia to take a course for my post-graduate degree but was seduced by the city and decided to stay."*

🔒 Secret Spot
— *Tiber Island*

This is one of my favorite spots in Rome, especially during the summer. I venture there in the early morning, usually alone. Everyone else there is just like me, Romans escaping the daily grind, seeking the magic spell of the golden rays of a glorious sun and a rare moment to think and dream.

♀ Favorite Bar
— *Settembrini*

Via Luigi Settembrini, 27

Hands down my favorite bar for breakfast and coffee, but I don't go there as often as I would like to. Their *cornetto*s are divine and not as greasy as the average ones. There is an absolutely gorgeous external seating area that adds to the charm on a perfect sunny day.

My secret to happiness:

"To always have a smile"

Marianna Forleo

Researcher

— *Originally from Puglia, now based in Rome, recommends...*

What do you like most about living in Rome?

> *I love the amazing climate, the diversity of people, and the mix of the provincialism and internationalism. Many people who live in Rome complain of getting jaded by the city's less accommodating features. But few, if any, ever leave."*

Favorite Restaurant
— *Romolo e Remo*

Via Pannonia, 22-26

Located in a neighborhood called Appio Latino, this restaurant is where I spend many evenings dining with my closest friends. The ambience is very Roman, which means very relaxed. If you like soccer, you will appreciate the numerous photos of famed Roma player Francesco Totti, who is reputed to drop in every now and then. Eat there to try typical Roman dishes without any pretentious or touristic slants.

Loving Rome
— *Ludovisi Battle*
sarcophagus

Made or Born Roman?

> *Born and raised in Rome, or una Romana vera as they say in Italian. My love for this city is reflected in my profession.''*

What do you like most about living in Rome?

> *I can't imagine living anywhere else but Rome. We have it all— culture, art, history, archaeology, fantastic weather, amazing food, friendly people. Even traffic, the bane of our existence, has its own charm! What's life without a little adrenalin to start your day?''*

🔒 Secret Spot
— *Vicolo del cinque*

I'm from the Trastevere neighborhood, which hides a plethora of amazing secret spots such as hidden squares, or just a tiny alleyway, which leads you to an even tinier passage. But my most intimate spot has to be at the intersection where *Vicolo del Cinque* and *Vicolo della Scala* meet. When I stand there, it's like I am under an invisible field of magic.

🍷 Favorite Bar
— *BArt Auditorium Parco della Musica*

Viale Pietro De Coubertin, 30

I have a serious allergy towards the bars in the center of Rome. Why pay three times for a cappuccino? This bar is not just good for great coffee, but a drink before your concert. For a reasonable set fee, they have an all-you-can-eat deal.

My secret to happiness:

"To go where my heart takes me"

Antonella Palma
Tour Guide

— *Born and raised in Rome, recommends...*

🍴 Favorite Restaurant
— *Il Condor*

Via Daniele Manin, 50

This is the antithesis of the tourist traps you'll find on the main squares. You'll be hard-pressed to find tourists here, but plenty of loud locals gesticulating with their hands as only Italians do best. Come here for the real-deal Roman fare, cooked with nothing but love.

My secret to happiness:

"To wind down in special places with the people dearest to me"

Francesca

Architect/Homemaker

— Born and bred in Rome, recommends...

Made or Born Roman?

I was born in Rome and have always lived here. When I was younger, I developed a travel bug and went across the world, but I knew then that Rome would always be my eternal home.

What do you like most about living in Rome?

I love how there's an infinite variety of things to do and see, be it on the culinary, cultural, or leisurely levels. It's the sort of city that always has the upper hand on you in terms of unexpected surprises. Just when you think you've seen the breadth of her beauty, she plays an unexpected hand."

 Favorite Restaurant
— Costanza Hostaria

Piazza del Paradiso, 65

This is my favorite restaurant in Rome, which I reserve for special occasions, or when I'm in the mood to stroll around the Campo de' Fiori area. Their signature dish has to be the Chateaubriand with mushroom sauce. It's right under the steps of Theatre of Pompeo, the first brick theatre built by the Romans in 55 A.D. With that sort of history surrounding you, a simple meal suddenly becomes more significant.

Secret Spot
— Trevignano Romano

A special place where I like to go to wind down with my family is a little town north of the city called Trevignano Romano. This historic hamlet is perched on a hill and overlooks the Bracciano Lake. Surrounded by an abundance of nature, the centerpiece of which is the lake, it's close enough for a day trip for tourists who want to see a different shade of beautiful Rome.

Favorite Bar
— Caffè Novecento

Via del Governo Vecchio, 12

There is no lack of tacky bars around the highly touristic Piazza Navona area, but this place is the exception. The combination of a refined ambience, high-quality pastries, and delicacies to go with perfect coffee is unique. Also splendid for an afternoon tea break.

Made or Born Roman?

♀ Favorite Bar
— *Panella*

Via Merulana, 54

Great coffee is abundant in Rome. But if you want to add a unique touch to your coffee ritual, this is the place to go. I go all out in my indulgence and add a bit of zabaione cream on my coffee. And if you want to totally live dangerously, their desserts will corrupt the incorruptible.

🔒 Secret Spot
— *Zibaldone di Cose*

A bit out of the ordinary probably, my secret spot is an atelier in the hip neighborhood of San Lorenzo. Prepare to run into young university students and extroverted artist types who tend to flock there. That said, this is my ideal oasis to escape Rome's hustle and bustle. I go there to get inpired.

My secret to happiness:
"To take life with a pinch of salt and be content with yourself"

Angela Colace

Lawyer

— *Born in Calabria, now based in Rome, recommends...*

What do you like most about living in Rome?

" I love the sense of eternity lingering around every corner, reminding you exactly how old this place is. I adore the morning light, the romantic sunrises, and walking around the historic center. This city is like no other, despite any day-to-day flaws."

 Favorite Restaurant
— *Club Machiavelli*

Via Machiavelli, 49

If you are into big, bold flavors like me, this place will rock your universe. Their house speciality is *pasta con guanciale e cipolle caramellate di tropea*, or pasta with bacon and caramelized onions of Tropea. The owner, Mauro, has become a friend since I eat there practically every day. The place has a homey feeling, which means many diners hang out long after they've eaten. You want to know how much I love this place? I hosted my wedding dinner there.

47

My secret to happiness:

"Hang out in the outdoors for most of the day"

Giacomo Bisanti

Scriptwriter

— *Born in Milan, based in Rome, recommends...*

🍴 Favorite Restaurant
— *Giulio Passami L'Olio*

Via di Monte Giordano, 28

Located in the lively Campo de' Fiori area, this place has a very young milieu. It's tiny on the inside, but has long outdoor tables that cater to a raucous evening crowd. The setting is so intimate and cozy, you invariably end up making friends with other diners. This is casual and affordable Roman food targeting the young crowd.

Made or Born Roman?

❝ I was born and bred in Milan but was seduced by Rome four years ago. I moved here and now call this beautiful city my home.❞

What do you like most about living in Rome?

❝ That you never get bored of this town. I wake up every day and fall in love with it for different reasons. Is it at times a challenge to navigate? Of course, but what major metropolitan center isn't. For its pains, Rome makes up for it by its eternal beauty.❞

🍷 Favorite Bar
— *La Zanzara*

Via Crescenzio, 84

Probably dating back to the early 1900s, this bar has a unique vibe to it. In the mornings it's all about delicious coffees and refined pastries and delicacies. From the late afternoon to the early evening, it caters to young professionals flocking in for a relaxing drink at the end of a very long and often grinding Roman day.

🔒 Secret Spot
— *Via Sacra*

This was the main thoroughfare of ancient Rome, from the top of the Capitoline Hill, through some of the most significant sacred sites of the Forum, hence its name: The Sacred Road. Today, not many people use this path to get to the Fori Imperiali, and hence its tranquility. I go there for one of the most spectacular views of this city.

Loving Rome
— *Villa Doria Pamphili*

Marzia Gandiglio

Researcher

— *Born in Turin, based in Rome, recommends...*

Made or Born Roman?

I was born in Turin but moved to Rome a long time ago, so I consider myself Roman by default.

Secret Spot
— *Sant'Onofrio al Gianicolo*

This is the official church of the papal order of knighthood Order of the Holy Sepulchre. A hidden treasure that's easy to miss but essential to visit. Seventeenth-century frescoes, a wall entombment with skulls and skeletons, a tiny garden with a fountain where you can sit to contemplate the spectacular view of Rome before you.

Favorite Bar
— *Bar Picchiotto*

Piazza di S. Cosimato, 33

I am always looking for less crowded places to drink, rest, or eat, and this bar is hidden in a back street off a quiet square. It's not very visible to pedestrians. It's my favorite bar for a chilled coffee and *cornetto* in the morning or a drink after a hard day at work.

Favorite Restaurant
— *Casa Bleve*

Via del Teatro Valle, 48

This is a quiet restaurant. Don't hate me, but because it's pricey, it discourages many people from dining there, which makes it more special. The food, of course, is the real star here.

What do you like most about living in Rome?

The atmosphere of this city is unique, especially for a non-Roman like myself. It's entirely outgoing, which for an extrovert like me is often needed to get me out of my element. Rome has taught me to adapt and coexist with others around me.

Favorite Restaurant
— *La Lampara a Fiumicino*

Lungomare Della Salute, 23, Fiumicino

The restaurant is technically in the Fiumicino area, out by the airport, but practically it's still Rome. This is a seafood place known for the fairest prices for the freshest fish. You will find a predominantly Italian clientele who are in the know about this well-kept secret. Go there to get the best fish soup you will ever have—I guarantee it.

Secret Spot
— *Villa Borghese*

I am pretty certain I won't be the only one to cite these magical gardens as my secret spot of choice. The Villa Borghese was built by the architect Flaminio Ponzio, completed by his assistant Giovanni Vasanzio. Now, granted, the entire place is special, but within the gardens is another secret—a field full of the most beautiful roses you will ever see.

Favorite Bar
— *Sant'Eustachio Il Caffè*

Piazza Sant'Eustachio, 82

Like all good Romans, drinking good coffee in a bar is an obligatory ritual. This bar is located in the historic center of the city and they take their coffee seriously, even by Italian standards. Whether it's just straight coffee or their Eustachio cappuccino topped with their delectable homemade cream, you'll only understand once you've tried it.

My secret to happiness:
"Writing. Through my words I am able to create my picture-perfect world"

Mauro Nobilia

Thinker

— *Born and bred in Rome, recommends…*

Made or Born Roman?

> *Not only am I a seventh-generation Roman, but I was born in the heart of the city.*

What do you like most about living in Rome?

> *I moved to the outskirts of the city to get away from the traffic and the chaos, but the irony is, now that I have the peace and quiet, I miss the hustle and bustle. Go figure. But when I crave it, I just hop into my car and drive straight to the noisiest, most chaotic parts of the city to soak it all up!*

Loving Rome
— *St. Peter's
Basilica*

Made or Born Roman?

> " *I was born in a town close to Rome, Latina, but moved to Rome to study architecture ten years ago and never left.* "

What do you like most about living in Rome?

> " *That's a difficult question to answer, but I am not being disingenuous when I say I love everything about Rome! Like any love relationship, you cannot expect perfection, but you must learn to accept and maybe even love your partner's defects. Rome has its fair share of those, but it's still exactly my type of city.* "

🔒 Secret Spot
— *Secret Café*

My secret little spot is adequately called Secret Café. If you can appreciate an urban oasis that allows you to recharge, relax, and listen to your own thoughts in your own time, then I highly recommend this place. It's tucked away in the famous San Giovanni Square.

🍷 Favorite Bar
— *33 Testaccio Loungebar*
Via di Monte Testaccio, 33

This is a bit of an elaborate take on the typical Roman coffee bar and is more suited for a late-morning brunch. If you love live music, you will appreciate the eclectic mix of rock or hip hop acts that often perform there. Not to mention that their menu is simply exceptional. Also a great option for early-evening drinks and serious after-hour outings.

My secret to happiness:

"To appreciate even the smallest things in life"

Giuseppe Salino

Architect

— *Born in Latina, now based in Rome, recommends...*

🍴 Favorite Restaurant
— *Felice*
Via Mastro Giorgio, 29

This could be one of the oldest restaurants in Rome, but certainly it's a timeless institution in the neighborhood of Testaccio, where it's located. I go there for their amazing Roman dishes. My mouth waters when I think of their pasta *cacio e pepe* (pecorino cheese and ground black pepper), which I think is the best in town. It could do with a bit of a facelift, but even with its vintage feel, the food and service speak for themselves.

51

My secret to happiness:

"To believe I already possess what I need to be happy"

Rossana Palescandolo

Pharmaceutical Representative

— Born and bred in Rome, recommends...

Favorite Restaurant
— *Trecca Bistrot*

Via Alessandro Severo, 222

When I think of typical Roman eateries off the touristic track, this place jumps to mind. In the heart of EUR, the newer part of Rome, this is modern Italian food at its best. Go more than once and you will be greeted by name and your order preferences recalled. My favorite dish is *coda alla vaccinara*, a contemporary Roman oxtail stew.

Made or Born Roman?

Not only was I born in Rome, but to a staunchly Roman family deeply rooted in this city. Being Roman is akin to my genetic constitution."

What do you like most about living in Rome?

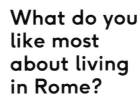

Unlike many cities in the world, the emphasis of living in Rome is 'Living.' It's a magical city that leaves you spellbound and unable to comprehend moving anywhere else. I was born here, but I understand why visitors would envy me."

Favorite Bar
— *Bar Trecastelli*

Via dei Georgofili, 91

I am not a chatterbox in the morning, and love it when I step in this bar, the baristas prepare the coffee they've named after me and leave it on the counter with a heart-shaped biscuit. Then, when I am coffeed-up and ready to chat, it's like I am in my own living room at home chatting with close friends and family. This is what makes Roman bars unique institutions.

Secret Spot
— *Gianicolo Hill*

The Gianicolo Hill is my favorite spot. When I am on top of it, inhaling the breathtaking views of the city, I feel that Rome is mine and mine alone. Standing there brings every facet of the city together in one overpowering emotion of love, loyalty, and a sense of belonging to something far bigger than me.

Secret Restaurant
— *Trecca Bistrot*

My secret to happiness:

"To do what I please when I please"

Alessandro Masi

Employee

— *Born in Bari and based in Rome, recommends...*

Made or Born Roman?

> *I was born and raised in Bari, in the region of Puglia. I moved to Rome to complete my education. It was many years before it dawned on me I was never going to leave."*

🔒 Secret Spot
— *Il Ghetto*

Rome is a virtual cornucopia of tiny alleyways, secret gardens, and oases tucked in the heart of the hustle and bustle. But if you like exceptionally secluded places for a reprieve, I would recommend any of the squares in the historic Jewish ghetto along the Tiber.

🍸 Favorite Bar
— *Checco er Carettiere*

Via Benedetta, 10

I am usually quite loyal when it comes to this bar, especially for breakfast. My mornings usually start slow, and the idea of having my coffee at an unknown bar and risk a lousy cappuccino is something I dread. This is why I simplify my life by going to the same excellent bar every morning, including Sunday!

🍴 Favorite Restaurant
— *Osteria Numero 6*

Via Garibaldi, 60

If you are more into protein and less into carbs, this restaurant will not disappoint you. The meat is excellent whether you like it rare, medium, or well done, although the latter will earn you the chagrin of the chef! The wine options are superb, also available by the glass, which means you can try more than one.

What do you like most about living in Rome?

> *I come from the South and found in Rome the same warmth of spirit, joy, and love of life I thought I would miss in my own hometown. Rome is a seductress—she quickly assimilates and adopts its newcomers to ensure it's impossible to leave."*

🔒 Secret Spot
— *Le domus Romane Di Palazzo Valentini*

These are archaeological remains of ancient Roman houses recently uncovered beneath Palazzo Valentini, now on permanent display, adding to Rome's already rich historical and artistic heritage. The ruins reveal an area that bridges the ancient, medieval, and modern topography of Rome. It's done exceptionally well—an incredible multimedia walk through history.

🍴 Favorite Restaurant
— *Enoteca Regionale Palatium*

Via Frattina, 94

This is one of my favorite places to eat in Rome. Many local restaurants focus on Roman fare, but the speciality here covers the entire region of Lazio. Simple, earthy flavors. Their house speciality is a pasta with chickpeas that I frequently dream of.

🍷 Favorite Bar
— *Caffè Capitolino*

Piazzale Caffarelli, 4

This bar is located on the top floor of the Capitolini Museum. Okay, so the coffee is outstanding, and the food is superb. But that's not hard to find in Rome. What sets this bar apart, however, is the stunning view of Rome. Enjoy your drink while absorbing every bit of the magical vista before you, especially at sunset.

Made or Born Roman?

❝ *I came here thirty-two years ago chasing my heart and my dreams. At first my work took me around the world, but Rome and motherhood changed my path.* ❞

My secret to happiness:
"To enjoy and cherish the small joys of life. A sunset, a hug, a smile..."

Mariarita Russo

Marketing and Communication Expert

— *Based in Rome, recommends...*

What do you like most about living in Rome?

❝ *The frenetic rhythm of everyday life has the tendency to gently overlap with the thrilling and breathtaking spots offered by the city. Rome's contrasting identities—ancient and omnipresent versus modern and transient, make it a very seductive place to call home.* ❞

Loving Rome
— *Ornate*
buildings

Made or Born Roman?

> *I am originally French but moved here for work. I had always wanted to live in Italy, and Rome specifically."*

 ## Secret Spot
— *Villa Torlonia*

I love walking and being one with nature. Rome is full of breathtaking villas and parks. Apart from the most famous ones like Villa Borghese, I particularly like Villa Torlonia. Originally designed by Giuseppe Valadier, the grounds were abandoned for a long time until a recent renovation opened it to the public. There's a small museum of private affects of the Torlonia family, who first commissioned it. Very easy to lose yourself there.

Favorite Bar
— *Freni e Frizioni*

Via Del Politeama, 4/6

It's almost impossible to find a mediocre coffee bar in Rome, so I'll tell you instead about my favorite cocktail bar in the Trastevere neighborhood. The hip, young, and beautiful flock here. This is the perfect spot for an evening *aperitivo* where you pay a set fee for one drink and finger food like delicious hummus, organic dips, and grilled veggies.

My secret to happiness:

"To appreciate the simplest, most accessible things"

Elena Dufour

Renewable Energy Guru

— *Born in France, now based in Rome, recommends...*

What do you like most about living in Rome?

> *The food is the biggest attraction here, followed closely by the incomparable beauty of the architecture and monuments. I am unable to resist walking into every church I come across, or to lose myself in the small alleyways of the historic center. There is always something new to discover, like hidden gardens and houses."*

 ## Favorite Restaurant
— *Osteria da Marcello*

Via dei Campani, 12

When I first dined at this place, we arrived early in the evening and it was practically empty. Thirty minutes later, there was a long line snaking outside, and for good reason. You will find here typical Roman food at fair prices and generous portions. My favorite dish is thinly sliced beef served with shaved parmesan and arugula. The restaurant is family owned, and often you can catch glimpses of the grand matriarch ruling the kitchen with an iron fist.

My
secret to
happiness:

*"Living
in Rome"*

Max Leotta

Tour Guide

— *Born and based in Rome,
recommends...*

Made or Born Roman?

🔒 Secret Spot
— *Gianicolo
Fountain*

The Gianicolo, but not the main square, because that's where every man and their dog flock to. Not many people know this, but the best spot is by the fountain, mainly because it's accessible only by foot and one of the few 'secret' spots in Rome where you don't feel like someone's squealed and let the cat out of the bag.

🍷 Favorite Bar
— *Sant'Eustachio
Il Caffè*

Piazza di Sant'Eustachio, 82

Like most Romans, I usually have breakfast at the bar underneath my house. When I'm pressed for time, I usually end up here late in the morning. They source their coffee from the city of Salerno, famous for its roast. This is a landmark bar in the city. Come here to taste decadent coffee with cream presented with flair.

🍴 Favorite Restaurant
— *Da Tonino*

Via del Governo Vecchio, 18-19

No matter how hard you try, you cannot end up in a more Roman restaurant than this one. Even the owners look like they stepped out of a black-and-white Italian movie set in this city. Unlike the minimalist decor and fair prices, the portions are abundant. The music is loud and lively. That doesn't bother me, and you'll learn to appreciate it, if only for the food.

What do you like most about living in Rome?

Made or Born Roman?

> *I was born and raised in the Piedmont region in northern Italy. I moved to Rome about ten years ago.*

What do you like most about living in Rome?

> *I love how green this city is. There are at least three or four large Central Park-style swathes of parkland that act as much needed oases from the chaos of the city. You really get the feeling that you are out of town there. But what good are parks if the weather is lousy? Rome is blessed with an ideal climate.*

🔒 Secret Spot
— *Parco della Caffarella*

This is a rather large park in the south of Rome, close to a metro stop. I love it because it feels like you are in the countryside, while still being on the outskirts of a major metropolitan center. Fortunately, it's protected from urban development because it comprises several major items of archaeological significance. There's a working farm on site, so it's great for kids. It's also an ecological treasure with about one hundred species of birds and fauna.

💡 Favorite Bar
— *Pasticceria Boccione*
Via del Portico D'Ottavia, 1

This pastry shop and bar is on a corner street in the Jewish ghetto of Rome. A landmark, it epitomizes the best of the Jewish traditions in Rome. It's bursting with character, grumpy old ladies, and colorful individuals who live in the area. You must try what they call a Jewish pizza, which is a sweet pastry that is a wonderful complement to the excellent coffee they serve.

My secret to happiness:

"My wife"

Lorenzo Casaccia

Engineer

— *Born in northern Italy, now lives in Rome, recommends...*

🍴 Favorite Restaurant
— *Emma Pizzeria*
Via del Monte della Farina, 28

Roscioli is one of the oldest bakeries operating in Rome. Recently, they opened this gourmet pizzeria in the heart of the city. Expect to pay a little more than your average mom and pop place, but it's well worth it. They have the classics and their own creations, like the Scozzese e Bufala pizza with fresh buffalo mozzarella from Paestum, Scottish salmon from Loch Fyne, wild fennel from Valentano, and wild arugula salad.

My secret to happiness:

"To stay optimistic and strive for good health"

Victor Colaiacomo

Tour Guide

— Born and based in Rome, recommends...

Made or Born Roman?

> *I was born and raised in Rome. Even though I work with tourists, my wanderlust desires are limited to visiting places, but never to leave my beautiful city."*

🔒 Secret Spot
— *Piazza Farnese*

This is one of Rome's most underrated squares. I make it a point to bring tourists here because, left to their own devices, it's unlikely they would hear of it. I also come here for my own leisure. It's open and spacious and allows you to lose yourself. Because it's not one of the more famous squares, you can still see indigenous Romans in their natural element.

💡 Favorite Bar
— *Josephine Bistrot*

Via Bissolati, 34

Most Romans are quite finicky about their coffee, but I'm more pedantic about my *cornetti*. If I stumble on a bad one when I'm venturing out to unknown bars out of necessity, my day is bound to be ruined. At this particular bar, I find they don't bake their pastries, they craft them with love, day in, day out. It goes without saying that their coffee is top-notch.

🍴 Favorite Restaurant
— *Osteria di Agrippa*

Via dei Cestari, 38

Imagine being invited by a Roman matriarch to savor her traditional fare, only the venue is in the center of historic Rome. Their pastas are all handmade, bursting with freshness. Don't leave Rome without trying their *carciofo alla giudia*—a Roman Jewish delicacy made of deep-fried whole artichokes.

What do you like most about living in Rome?

> *My job makes me interact quite a lot with tourists, but also with true Romans and I tell you, with a few exceptions, Romans are always ready to help and make you feel at home, while cracking deadpan jokes that leave you in stitches. I think of Rome as a big home with a bigger heart."*

My secret to happiness:

"The small pleasures and moments of life"

Lorenzo Baccin

CEO Romeloft.com

— Born and based in Rome, recommends...

Made or Born Roman?

🔒 Secret Spot
— *Piazza Venezia Parks*

This quiet spot is a beautiful garden hidden in the middle of the chaotic Piazza Venezia. I love the peaceful atmosphere and the elegant architecture. There is also a summer program of events in the garden with festivals, art exhibitions and theater performances.

🍷 Favorite Bar
— *Antico Bar Pasticceria Mariani*

Via dei Pettinari, 44

This cozy family run bar is home to the friendliest barista in Rome and the strongest coffee I've found. They also have a great selection of little biscuits and cakes to enjoy with your coffee. It's right next to Ponte Sisto, across the river from Trastevere, making it a perfect after lunch spot.

🍴 Favorite Restaurant
—*Emma Pizzeria*

Via del Monte della Farina, 28

This gourmet pizzeria in Campo de' Fiori uses organic and seasonal ingredients to make their delicious signature pizza and focaccia. It has a pretty outside terrace which is perfect for warm summer evenings. When you think of a Roman pizzeria, you typically think of a rowdy, cheap and cheery family run place. This place is far from it, because it takes the traditional Roman pizza concept and elevates to new, delicious heights. You will absolutely not regret it.

What do you like most about living in Rome?

This city has the most beautiful light in the world. My favorite time of day is toward the end of the afternoon, when the sun starts to set and the monuments begin to glow with early evening light. I guarantee that the best director of photography in the world can never recreate this magic."

Secret Spot
— *Pantheon*

Most people visit the Pantheon only a few times in their lives. I'm fortunate to work in an office that's a few steps from there, which means most of my coffee breaks are always around it. Essentially, any opportunity to go there, I usually grab it. I mostly sit by the fountain stairs and enjoy the view of the church and the scenic buildings that surround it.

Favorite Bar
— *Bar Totó*

Via del Portico D'Ottavia, 2

I live in the Jewish Ghetto and know each and every corner of the area. This by far is my favorite bar there, engraved with so much history and tradition. Go there to see locals getting their morning coffee, an afternoon cocktail, or an evening espresso enhanced with a shot of liquor.

Made or Born Roman?

66 I was born and raised in Rome and feel fortunate that I work and live in the historic center. I'm your classic Roman who wouldn't dream of any other city as a home."

What do you like most about living in Rome?

66 I love the sense of security I have living in Rome. You never feel lonely here, surrounded by diverse people who constitute the core of the unique Roman lifestyle. Despite the history, the city is alive and in perpetual motion."

My secret to happiness:

"Remaining tolerant and accepting of others"

Luciana Cannistra

Librarian

— *Born in Viterbo, now based in Rome, recommends...*

Favorite Restaurant
— *Enoteca Spiriti*

Piazza di Pietra, 32/33

If, like me, you are picky about raw fish, then this is the restaurant for you. The dishes are exceptionally simple, but the quality of their ingredients is out of this world. I am certain that they don't even own a deep freezer. You'll find me there having lunch at least three to four times a week, with colleagues and girlfriends. I highly recommend the *carpaccio di manzo* (beef carpaccio), which is deliciously prepared and presented.

Secret Spot
— *Castel,
Sant'Angelo*

Made or Born Roman?

 I was born in a town close to Rome called Viterbo, but moved to Rome when I was a kid and stayed here thereafter."

 Secret Spot
— *Piazza Trilussa*

Tucked in the Trastevere neighborhood, this is definitley my favorite secret spot in Rome. I recommend going there to experience the essence of a Roman piazza and absorb the city's best vibes. Trastevere in general, and this spot in particular, invokes the spirit of a self-contained village within the heart of the city. And it's far more than the bars and restaurants in the square, but the sort of typical Roman faces you will see there that make it special.

Favorite Bar
— *Il Cornettone*

Via Nettunense Nuova, 10

The name of the bar says it all. I go there for their delicious and oversized *cornetto*s. Though delicious in its own right, coffee in this bar plays second fiddle to the pastries, which are by far the main attraction. I usually have a frothy cappuccino or an espresso to start my day.

My secret to happiness:

"Work hard to understand what happiness really is"

Fabio Confli

Computer Programmer

— *Born in Viterbo, now based in Rome, recommends...*

What do you like most about living in Rome?

Rome has a lot to offer in terms of activities, stemming from its proud history, gorgeous climate, and rich culture. It's a city that inspires you to live it to its full potential and discover new things at your leisure. And the more you see of it, the more you fall in love with Rome."

Favorite Restaurant
— *Hostaria da Nerone*

Via delle Terme di Tito, 96

If you are looking to spend a little more for quality dining, then this is the best place in town to do just that. They have the best Roman-style pizza—thin and crunchy. Run by a rather large family, the vibe is casual and friendly. It is not uncommon for the regulars to find plates they didn't order appearing on their table, on the house. I go there all seasons, while their cosy garden exemplifies the best of the *vita Trasteverina*—the Trastevere neighborhood lifestyle.

Castel Sant'Angelo
Rome, 6.50 am

My secret to happiness:

"To have a squeaky-clean conscience"

Amleto Frisani

Retiree

— Born in Taranto, now lives in Rome, recommends...

Made or Born Roman?

I am originally from Taranto, in the beautiful region of Puglia. I moved to Rome about twenty-six years ago. While I consider myself to be part Roman, my roots will always be in Puglia."

Favorite Bar
— Doney Café

Via Vittorio Veneto, 137-141

An exceptionally elegant bar that caters mainly to mature clientele like myself. Still, no matter how old you are, this is a must-visit bar if you want to soak in the typical Roman coffee culture. Regulars like me are treated like royalty. My coffee and a slice of Roman-style apple pie materialize even before I utter a word. Despite its prime location, their prices are very fair.

Secret Spot
— Celio

This is one of the seven hills upon which Rome was founded. Its beauty stems from being in the midst of the most important Roman treasures, such as the Colosseum. No matter how blue you are feeling, or how rambunctious this naughty little town can get, a few hours in this area is like a balm for the heart and soul. Timeless history puts everything in perspective.

Favorite Restaurant
— Pollarola

Piazza Pollarola, 25

A small gem. It's imperative to make a reservation to avoid disappointment. The food is authentic and cooked with pride and craft. Their wine selection is intelligent, even the humble house is full-bodied and satisfying. I would recommend the artichokes cooked Roman style. Best of all, their menu is ever-evolving.

What do you like most about living in Rome?

That's easy. I love the Romans. I was raised in Taranto, but the citizens of this city adopted me and made me one of their own. Despite their seemingly hard exterior, Romans are as soft as butter on the inside and once you get to know them, they cherish you for life."

My secret to happiness:

"To look in the mirror and be content with what I see"

Valeria Cappelletti

Woman of Leisure

— Born and based in Rome, recommends...

Made or Born Roman?

🔒 Secret Spot
— *Vicolo Moroni*

Walking around Rome's tiniest and most secluded alleyways is the best way to keep falling in love with the city. This particular one in Trastevere is magical and feels like time stood there. I find it incredible that no matter how many tourists descend on this city, you can still find a spot like this for some solitude and mental rejuvenation.

🍷 Favorite Bar
— *Aristocampo*

Piazza della Cancelleria, 93

I am shamelessly promiscuous when it comes to a morning coffee bar. I usually just go down to my neighborhood bar for a cappuccino and a *cornetto*, often on the go. However, I do extend some loyalty to this place where I have my afternoon coffee or evening *aperitivo*. The bar and the location are hip and wild, just like me, as evident from my hair!

🍴 Favorite Restaurant
— *Sapore di Mare*

Via del Piè di Marmo, 36

I love seafood over pizza and pasta. I've tried them all and this one is by far the very best. From the minute you step in, you know you are in for a treat. Warm faces and honest smiles welcome you, along with the mouthwatering aromas of grilled fish in the air. The portions are not huge, so ladies, make sure you go with a generous date so you can order enough until you leave satisfied. It's also not the cheapest joint in town.

What do you like most about living in Rome?

I love Rome for its sort of beauty that never grows old. You can never tire of the city or feel like you want to cheat on her for any extended period of time. Even when I travel to the most beautiful cities in the world, I appreciate them for what they are, but always end up itching to get back to my beautiful city."

 ## Favorite Bar
— *Bar del Fico*

Piazza del Fico, 26

This is one of Rome's most trendy and lively haunts, but not in an over-the-top way. You will find a rich mix of clientele across a very diverse age group, but the one thing they all have in common is being edgy and stylish. The ultimate coffee experience is their cappuccino topped with their homemade cream. Mmmm, I can just taste it!

Secret Spot
— *Parco Savello*

This park is known for its glorious panoramic views of Rome and its quiet and romantic setting. I usually go in the early afternoon hours to fully enjoy Rome looking back at me at that particular part of the day, with hardly anyone in sight. This, followed by a nice brisk walk, is the best way to prep yourself for a wild Roman night out.

My secret to happiness:
"To live peacefully, and to live freely..."

Made or Born Roman?

> *I am originally Israeli, but moved to Rome about five years ago to study. You can think of me now as an Isratalian!"*

Ham

Speech Therapy Student

— *Born in Israel, studying in Rome, recommends...*

What do you like most about living in Rome?

> *Rome is not a city you can love at all times. Maybe most of the time, but not always. On the good days when the sun is shining and you have a day off all to yourself, Rome is an open air museum, or even a small village where everyone is by default on leisurely mode. You eat well, you drink well, and you make fantastic friends. What more could you ask for?"*

 ## Favorite Restaurant
— *Bella Carne*

Via del Portico D'Ottavia, 51

This must-try place is in the heart of the Jewish quarter in Rome, the ghetto. Jewish influence on Roman cuisine is vast and gave us the world-famous, highly decadent fried whole artichokes. This is a kosher grill, where the quality of the meats and the pastas is beyond this world. Like most restaurants in the ghetto, space is a premium so you would be better served to reserve in advance. They also have some Israeli favorites like hummus and falafel, so I go there when I am homesick.

Secret Spot
— *Via Giulia*

Made or Born Roman?

" *I was born in Rome, right behind the famous Campo de' Fiori. I have lived in the same area for the last seventy plus odd years.*

What do you like most about living in Rome?

" *Rome allows you to do, say, and think anything you want. You can misbehave in public every once in a while, and the city and the public are magnanimous enough to forgive you. There are rules, of course, black and white, but the grey zone here gives us space to breathe, which for a city like Rome is a safety-valve."*

 Secret Spot
— *Via Giulia*

Most people only know this street as the secret spot behind Camp de Fiori where you used to be able to park for free, before the traffic police honed in on it. But it's actually one of the few streets that still maintains the look-and-feel and spirit of ancient Rome. Because there's very little commercial activity on it, you can enjoy a peaceful, reflective walk or marvel at the architecture.

 Favorite Bar
— *Bar Farnese*

Via Dei Baullari, 106

No doubt one of the best bars in Rome. It's been around for at least fifty years, and it's still Angelo, the owner, who prepares the coffee for regulars like me. Despite now being on the tourist map, none of that has fazed or changed them. The best coffee served with the best cream at the fairest prices.

My secret to happiness:
"Fresh water, pure wine, and beautiful women"

Gianfranco Angeli

Retired Lawyer

— *Born in Viterbo, now based in Rome, recommends...*

 Favorite Restaurant
— *Baffetto 2*

Piazza del Teatro di Pompeo, 18

Extremely simple, yet extremely delicious. Don't be fooled by lavish décor or famous restaurants with ridiculously expensive prices in Rome. The best food is found in joints like this. There is very little food styling that goes into their cooking, and that's because the ingredients and flavors need no gimmicks. Classics like *la gricia* pasta made with smoked pancetta and sheep cheese, or the quintessentially Roman pasta with *amatriciana* sauce, are some of their signature dishes.

My secret to happiness:

"To never take my good health for granted"

Chiara Francavilla

Unemployed

— Born in Palermo, now based in Rome, recommends...

Made or Born Roman?

66 *I was born in Palermo and moved to Rome to study twelve years ago. It was tough to start as I longed for my southern roots, but Rome eventually took me in and made me feel welcome."*

🔒 Secret Spot
— *Piazza Venezia Parks*

These stretches of green around one of the most iconic Roman squares are one of the city's best-kept secrets. It's known mostly to the locals who live in the neighborhood, and by word of mouth among university students. This is the very definition of an oasis, where you can escape the madness of Rome by day. Great for kids as well with a well-maintained playground.

🍷 Favorite Bar
— *Bar Frattina*

Via Frattina, 142

Any day that starts with breakfast at this bar is one I know will be good. A cappuccino or an espresso with a warm *cornetto* is what I love there. But coffee and pastries aside, their gelato is a notch above the rest with a huge variety of flavors. A true sign you are becoming a real Roman is when you start appreciating gelato in winter more than during the warmer months of spring and summer.

🍴 Favorite Restaurant
— *Ristorante Sugo*

Viale Angelico, 64

I love their constantly evolving menu, and the rich variety of their offerings without losing the plot. Service is friendly and from the heart. Often I feel like I am eating at my mother's table when I am there. Unlike the majority of Roman eateries, the portions here are very generous. My favorite item on the menu is the *spaghetti alle vongole* (clams).

What do you like most about living in Rome?

66 *Rome is a perpetually romantic city, despite many of its shortcomings. Few cities in the world are this good looking, or with this much character at any time of the day. To fall in love with Rome, all you have to do is just show up. Every corner, fountain, sculpture, and square infuses your heart with love for the city and for life."*

> *I was born in Portugal but moved to Rome twelve years ago. A Roman woman stole my heart and I decided I would stay to chase after. I never left."*

What do you like most about living in Rome?

> *Being southern European, Rome feels like home. Every face I come across on the street feels like someone I've hung out with before, or would love to hang out with. When you live here long enough, the warmth and familiarity that abound become indispensable and a part of your identity."*

My secret to happiness:

"To continuously evolve and set new targets for myself"

Pedro Guerra

Network Marketer

— Born in Portugal, now based in Rome, recommends...

 ### Secret Spot
— *Viale Europa*

In the heart of the new part of Rome and developed by Mussolini, this street is one of the best-kept secrets of people in the know. Like an oasis away from the craziness of the historic center, you'll find stylish but affordable shopping, a few very quaint coffee bars, and a 24-hour pharmacy. But the best part is people-watching. When you're done, there's a nearby park overlooking a lake where you can have a delicious gelato while lazing on the lawn.

 ### Favorite Bar
— *Il Gianfornaio*

Largo Apollinaire, 5/7

Their bakery and pastry shop is simply divine. They have the best *cornetti*, served warm and stuffed with homemade jams. Their portions are extremely generous. I guarantee you will go back more than once for their delicious pastries, even though they are on the pricey side. Their slogan says it all: "Our bread is more delicious than bread."

 ### Favorite Restaurant
— *Geco*

Piazza Guglielmo Marconi, 23

I prefer restaurants with open buffets or tapas where you can taste many things rather than gorge on a few big plates. This place is perfect for that. It's big, modern, and always with lively music piping in the background. The crowd there is mostly young and fashionable. If you don't want to move around on your night out, this is great for eating and then staying for drinks, and after a certain hour, dancing!

IL NOSTRO PANE È PIÙ BUONO DEL PANE.

My secret to happiness:

"To be healthy"

Luciano Preziosi

Taxi Driver

— *Born and raised in Rome, recommends...*

Made or Born Roman?

Born, bred, and raised Roman. If there is a blood test for Roman pedigree, my results would be off the charts."

🔒 Secret Spot
— *Villa Sciarra*

My secret oasis is located between Trastevere, Gianicolo, and Monteverde Vecchio. When I have a free moment during the day, I like to grab a quick bite to eat and enjoy some solitude in this beautiful park. It is quite secluded and not many people know about it, so the chance of being pestered by a rowdy bunch of people is roughly less than zero.

🏆 Favorite Bar
— *Cattive Compagnie*

Via Goffredo Mameli, 15

This bar is really ideal for a quick breakfast because they prepare the best coffees in the world at record speed. They know me by name and my bad habits, like always running late for work! I walk in and my coffee is ready on the counter, with the most delicious *cornetti* packed in a takeaway paper bag.

🍴 Favorite Restaurant
— *Popi Popi*

Via delle Fratte di Trastevere, 45

I suggest you make a reservation to avoid disappointment. Go there to try the best Roman-style pizza—thin, crunchy, and with the freshest ingredients. If you don't fancy what's on the menu, they'll custom-make one for you with your own toppings. I love the tuna and zucchini pizza.

Everything. Given my job, I get to enjoy this city to its full potential, especially at night when the traffic has waned and the monuments are beautifully lit, revealing the most enchanting Roman secrets."

What do you like most about living in Rome?

My secret to happiness:

"Spending time facing the sea to find my peace"

Stefania Farinelli

Housewife

— *Born and bred in Rome, recommends...*

Made or Born Roman?

❝ *My parents hailed from the region of Emilia-Romagna. They moved to Rome for work and had me here. They never went back, and I now consider myself one hundred percent Roman."*

🔒 Secret Spot
— *MAXXI Museum*

This museum is in the Flaminio area north of Rome. Whenever I have a few free hours and need to lose myself or to refuel on inspiration, I escape there. I switch my phone off and immerse myself and my senses in whatever is on display in the way of contemporary or edgy art. Designed by the late Iraqi-British architect Zaha Hadid, every visit is a delicious meal for the soul, and a refreshing contrast to the 'oldness' of Rome.

🍷 Favorite Bar
— *Bakery House*

Corso Trieste, 157b/c

I like my cappuccino to be very foamy, and many bars either give you too little or far too much. This is the only bar I know of in Rome that has mastered the art of the perfect froth, and they are pretty consistent about it. And they don't call themselves the Bakery House for no good reason. Their pastries are a notch above the run-of-the-mill Roman bar.

🍴 Favorite Restaurant
— *Dolce*

Via Tripolitania, 4

This place has a particular focus on desserts, and that's what I love about it. On Sundays, this is one of the few joints that does a breakfast-brunch type affair from eight until midday. Their desserts are mouthwatering. The interior design and vibe is stylish and original. My favorite indulgence is the *semi-freddo ai frutti di bosco* (semi-freddo with berries).

What do you like most about living in Rome?

❝ *I love that we enjoy a ridiculously rich quality of life, and it takes very little effort or preparation to bask in it. You wake up and the weather is warm and the sun is glorious above the sky. On a whim, you decide to start your day in the center of Rome with a breakfast overlooking any one of its beautiful squares."*

Made or Born Roman?

> *If it is not obvious from my thick Roman accent, I am as Roman as Julius Caesar. But unlike many people of my generation, I know my city and its heritage. I don't just live here, I am this city."*

🔒 Secret Spot
— *Porta Settimiana*

This is one of the gates of the Aurelian walls in the area of Trastevere, built by Emperor Aurelian in the third century. I love Trastevere in general because of its unique architecture, and the fact that it's not a museum, but a living, breathing village of true Romans. Artists and creative souls flock to it. When I am at the Porta Settimania, I just amble around or stand still to watch the rich tapestry of faces pass me by.

🍷 Favorite Bar
— *Caffè San Cosimato*

Piazza di San Cosimato, 61-62

Their selection of pastries leaves you speechless, but you can't leave this city without trying the *maritozzo alla panna*, a typical dessert of the region of Lazio. A soft bun made of pine nuts, raisins, and candied orange peel, stuffed with fresh whipped cream. Imagine that with one of the best cappuccinos in the world and the word heavenly comes to mind.

My secret to happiness:
"To keep laughing as long as you can"

Paolo Vanni

Unemployed

— *Born in Viterbo, now based in Rome, recommends...*

What do you like most about living in Rome?

> *Rome's many hidden secrets. For instance, many people don't know where the famous Tre Scalini (the three steps) bar in Piazza Navona gets its name. Legend has it that hundreds of years ago, the pope overheard a commoner criticizing his papacy. He ordered his head chopped off on the spot, and it rolled down three steps. It remained there for days until friends of the deceased retrieved the head, encased it in granite, and erected it on top of the building, where even today only a few people know of it."*

Favorite Restaurant
— *Ai Spaghettari*

Piazza di San Cosimato, 58

I eat out often to meet intelligent and interesting people, who as it were, tend to flock to places where you find exceptional food. Located in the heart of Trastevere, this is my go-to place for authentic Roman food that is loaded with flavor, crafted with love, and served with zero attitude. Run by a large family, you can glimpse the grandmother in the kitchen preparing the cakes or the grandfather washing the dishes. The pasta with carbonara sauce is a Roman staple, and they cook up a pretty amazing version of it.

Favorite
Restaurant
— *Piperno*

Made or Born Roman?

Proudly born and raised in Rome. If one could predetermine where they would be born, I don't think I could have improved on this."

🔒 Secret Spot
— *Via Piccolomini*

This road is perfectly aligned to the dome of St. Peter. Not many people know about it, but you experience a visual effect when you ride your motorcycle or drive your car towards the basilica at high speed. The closer you get to it, the further away the basilica appears to be. It's a freak of nature, but remarkably beautiful to experience. Every time I go through it, my spirits are lifted. It's also a great place for visitors who want to see something off the guidebook track.

🍷 Favorite Bar
— *Dadò Chalet*

Via Sabiniano, 30

The coffee is great but the cappucino is even better. This is not your regular Roman bar because it's located inside an elevated park with spectacular views of St. Peter's dome. During winter the bar is intimate, but during summer the atmosphere transforms and becomes more lively, with great music and outdoor seating.

My secret to happiness:

"The sun and the one I love"

Raffaele Fiorenza

Student

— Born and raised in Rome, recommends...

What do you like most about living in Rome?

The amazing weather. The climate is ideal. The city is breathtaking—I discover something new each time I step out of my house, almost like visiting a new city each time. Sure there's plenty of urban mayhem around here but it's also unique. There is no other city like Rome in the world. Just ask the tourists who lust after it."

🍴 Favorite Restaurant
— *Piperno*

Via Monte Dè Cenci, 9

My favorite dish is filetto di *baccalá fritto* (fried cod fillets). I usually dine at this restaurant for special occasions and when I want a guaranteed high quality-meal. It's absolutely amazing with a magical atmosphere, located in the picturesque Jewish ghetto.

A city of recognizable icons,
Rome, 7.12 pm

My secret to happiness:

"To be surrounded by eternal optimists"

Barbara

Home Chef

— *Born and raised in Rome, recommends...*

Made or Born Roman?

I am not only Roman, but an eighth-generation one. That's one generation more than what is strictly required to be considered a real Roman."

🔒 Secret Spot
— *Il Chiostro del Bramante*

This was formerly a convent designed by the famous fifteenth-century architect Bramante, near Piazza Navona. A spectacular, magical spot you have to visit to truly appreciate. On the first floor, despite being in the heart of Rome and overlooking Rome's rooftops, there's an indescribable silence and peaceful sense. Superbly charming.

🍷 Favorite Bar
— *Ombre Rosse*

Piazza di Sant'Egidio, 12-13, Rome

Going to this bar is as close as you can get to going to the beach in the heart of the city. You sit on big, comfy lounge chairs overlooking a bustling square filled with a sea of beautiful people strolling by. Sipping on a strong coffee with frothy milk in hand, you nibble on some delicious pastry. It's very hard to imagine how you can have a better breakfast.

🍴 Favorite Restaurant
— *Osteria da "Zi" Umberto*

Piazza di S. Giovanni della Malva, 14

Located in the Trastevere neighborhood, this restaurant draws me because of its delicious plates that I am unable to cook up myself. Especially *la coda alla vaccinara*, a modern Roman oxtail stew. This restaurant has mastered the art of preparing and serving it. My parents were butchers, and in my youth, I never wanted to eat meat as a form of rebellion against their profession. While I don't eat much meat now, this restaurant is where I allow myself to be corrupted.

What do you like most about living in Rome?

The rooftops. When I walk in Rome, I love looking at roof-tops. I admire the terraces, the architecture, the colors. Then, of course, I bump into things and people. Oh yes, people. They're the second thing I love most about Rome."

Made or Born Roman?

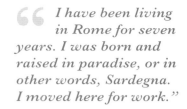

"I have been living in Rome for seven years. I was born and raised in paradise, or in other words, Sardegna. I moved here for work."

Secret Spot
— *Campo de' Fiori*

It's hardly a secret spot since it's probably one of the most visited squares in Rome. It's especially loved for its seemingly endless nightlife and boisterous fun. In the mornings, there is a fantastic market, not just of knickknacks, but good quality produce. Even if I am on my own, I love this square because it attracts big groups of friends of different ages, nationalities, tastes, and outlook. You feel alive just walking around and observing.

Favorite Bar
— *Sant'Eustachio Il Caffè*

Piazza di Sant'Eustachio, 82

If you find yourself walking on Via del Corso, stop at this bar to refuel with what I can boldly claim is the tastiest coffee in Rome. Their flagship beverage is Il Gran caffe. Coffees and pastries aside, I love how this bar is buzzing with interesting, quirky people in the mood to socialize.

My secret to happiness: *"Never to lose hope"*

Franco Guerra

Employee

— *Born in Sardegna, now based in Rome, recommends...*

Favorite Restaurant
— *Ristorante a Trastevere da Massi*

Via Della Scala, 34

The carbonara and the amatriciana pasta sauces are the epitome of Roman cuisine. You can't visit this city and leave without trying both. On a cold winter day or on a pleasant spring evening during a weekday to avoid the risk of not finding a table, head to this restaurant and prepare to be enthralled. A good plate of pasta is more than just the right flavors and craft, but where you eat it. And it doesn't get better than this place. Mostly adults there with hardly a screaming kid in sight!

What do you like most about living in Rome?

While Rome is best enjoyed by a tourist who is sheltered from its traffic, bureaucracy, and other challenges, what I love most is the ability to once in a while live like a traveler. To forget what I dislike about it most, and bask in its glory, history, and charm. A good coffee, a good bowl of pasta, or a pleasant walk go a long way in exonerating the city of its sins."

Made or Born Roman?

> *Born and raised in Rome, despite the fact I've always felt a deep urge to live elsewhere, like London. But I am still here."*

Secret Spot
— *Piazza Margana*

I will give you my secret spot, hoping by doing so I won't ruin it for the rest of us! This lovely square is really not easy to find. It was named after a powerful medieval family that had a main residence there. It feels like a small village that has remained unchanged for centuries. Few tourists venture there, so it's definitely my personal mental oasis.

Favorite Bar
— *Bar San Calisto*

Piazza di San Calisto, 4

Like most good Romans, I rarely have breakfast at home. I wake up, step out, and walk a few meters to this local bar. They know me by name, and have been fully briefed exactly how I take my coffee. By the time I salute the owner behind the till, my coffee is waiting for me on the counter. If I am working from home, I often take a few coffee breaks there too.

Paolo Biamonte

Music Critic

— *Born and raised in Rome, recommends...*

What do you like most about living in Rome?

> *I love Rome for what it stands for: the history, the culture, and the architecture. I like it a little less when it comes to living here on a daily basis. Just to get around the city or run basic errands can be a struggle. That said, most people like me are able to accept the city's waywardness because of how beautiful it is. Seems like a fair trade-off."*

Favorite Restaurant
— *Paris*

Via Piazza di San Calisto, 7/A

While the fare here is typically Roman, the ambience is far from it. The setting is quite elegant and you will be spared the chaos of a classic Roman mom and pop restaurant. The exquisite presentation of the food is your first clue this place is special. They have a vast and refined wine selection. Budget wise, this is not for the faint of heart, but you will not break the bank either to dine there.

Loving Rome
— *A city of iconic symbols*

Made or Born Roman?

> *My father is from Turkish Cyprus and my mother is Scottish. They moved to Rome and had me, so I am born Roman, but of non-Italian heritage.*"

What do you like most about living in Rome?

> *The laissez-faire, laidback way of life is a great match for my character. I love that nothing here is ever a problem. Nowhere is the edict 'hakuna matata' more applicable than in this town. Don't get me wrong, there are rules and regulations, but they are not always shoved down your throat.*"

🔒 Secret Spot
— *Arch of Janus*

This is the only four-faced triumphal arch preserved in Rome, in the Velabrum-Forum Boarium. It's within walking distance from my office, and sometimes I take a simple lunch and eat there when I want to reflect or need some quiet time. It's absolutely beautiful, you can't miss it.

🍸 Favorite Bar
— *Yellow Bar*

Viale Aventino, 78

Not too far from Circus Maximus, I love this bar because it does double duty as a great coffee bar for a morning breakfast or an espresso after lunch, as well as being a great choice for a drinking bar. Their beer is cold, their beer is cheap, and their beer is good.

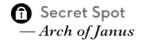

My secret to happiness:

"To wake up in the morning and I'm still alive"

Martin Hilmi

Enterprise Development Officer

— *Born and bred in Rome, recommends...*

🍴 Favorite Restaurant
— *Hostaria Da Corrado*

Via della Pelliccia, 39

This is your archetypal Roman dining experience, including the rude waiter. He'll often tell you we can't order 'that' because it will take too long to prepare, so order 'this' instead! But that's quite irrelevant, because everything they cook there is absolutely divine. I go there for the *bucatini all'amatriciana* (bucatini pasta with amatriciana sauce).

My secret to happiness:

"Music and motorcycles and mouthwatering food"

Bruno Casaregola

Surgeon

— *Born in Gaeta, now based in Rome, recommends...*

 Favorite Restaurant
— *La Taverna de' Mercanti*

Via Piazza dè Mercanti, 3A, Roma

My standard for the perfect restaurant is not just about the quality of the food, but the ambience has to be special because I like to feed my soul while I feed my belly. This restaurant is located in the vibrant neighborhood of Trastevere and is probably no less than three hundred years old. It's located on three floors and is very cozy with an open wood-fire grill and decorated with ancient Roman motifs like salvaged parts of chariots. Their meat is succulent and cooked perfectly. I highly recommend their Chateaubriand steak. Other Roman classics like artichokes and tripe are also crafted with love, and their wine selection is dizzying.

What do you like most about living in Rome?

" *I have a strong feeling of connection to this city. I belong to Rome and Rome belongs to me. Whenever I see Roman temples or ruins, I get goosebumps. It almost feels like I was here two thousand years ago. I feel I am the continuation of this heritage. Maybe it's a sort of genetic memory.*"

Made or Born Roman?

" *I was born in the lovely seaside town of Gaeta south of Rome. I moved to the city for a degree in medicine. My profession took me around the world, but I was ultimately seduced by Rome again.*"

 **Secret Spot**
— *Basilica Santo Stefano Rotondo*

Located in Celio, one of the seven ancient hills upon which the ancient city of Rome was founded, this church is so particularly enchanting that it's where I got married. It's round-shaped, probably built on an ancient Roman market. Frescoes on the walls depict martyrdom in Christianity. Beautifully haunting.

 **Favorite Bar**
— *Dagnino*

Via Vittorio Emanuele Orlando, 75, Roma

This bar is located in the Galleria Esedra off Piazza della Repubblica square. They specialize in Sicilian delicacies, specifically from Palermo. Go there for the very best *arancini*, *cassate siciliane*, and cannoli. The coffee is of course spectacular, but their real pièce de résistance is their mind-boggling selection of Sicilian ice cream.

Made or Born Roman?

> *Born in Rome to a Roman father and a mother from the city of Bari in the beautiful region of Puglia.*

🔒 Secret Spot
— *Beaches of Anzio*

I am a bit of a romantic and being at university for most of the week, whenever I have a free minute for myself, I jump on my scooter and head out to the beach in Anzio near Rome. I love sitting on the sand and watching the waves as they gently lap up to my feet. These are the cleanest and most picturesque beaches near Rome.

🍷 Favorite Bar
— *Rock Art Club*

Viale Luigi Fincati, 26

This is not your usual bar but a recreational center with craft beers and board games—yes, board games! I spend the best times ever there with my friends, especially after a tough week studying. Their choice of music is wicked, and best of all, it's tiny and never crowded.

My secret to happiness:

"Eating well and painting"

Elena Pio

Student

— *Born and based in Rome, recommends...*

What do you like most about living in Rome?

> *For a fine arts student, Rome is the picture-perfect city, full of monuments, fountains, incredible architecture, and museums. Not to mention incredible and incomparable cuisine. What more could one ask for?*

🍴 Favorite Restaurant
—*Molo 29*

Via Mario Musco, 29

Even though it is not a restaurant overlooking the sea, that hasn't stopped them from being one of the best seafood restaurants I've tried in Rome. Everything they prepare is delicious but my favorite is something I doubt most people have ever heard of or tried—*capesante in conchiglia.* This is basically scallops mixed with anchovies, onions, topped with breadcrumbs, and served in a shell. Just describing it makes my mouth water!

My secret to happiness:

"To love unconditionally"

Roberto Fagiani

Retailer

— Born and bred in Rome, recommends...

Made or Born Roman?

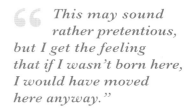

> *This may sound rather pretentious, but I get the feeling that if I wasn't born here, I would have moved here anyway."*

🔒 Secret Spot
— *Villa Torlonia*

One of Rome's most charming perks as a city is the abundance of green spaces. For a sports addict like myself who likes to stay fit and active, there is no better spot than Villa Torlonia. Whether it's a picturesque bike ride, or a tranquil spot for a workout or some tai chi, I always come here knowing I will leave feeling a little bit more alive.

🍷 Favorite Bar
— *Caffè San Cosimato*

Piazza di San Cosimato, 61-62

I get attached more to people rather than places. While this bar is blessed with one of the hottest locations a bar can ask for in the heart of Trastevere, I keep coming back for the service—always a smiling face, a coffee served just right, and a tradition of quality that can turn any bad day better.

🍴 Favorite Restaurant
— *Isola d'Oro*

Via della Scafa, 164, Fiumicino

Being health conscious, I am more likely to lunch on a baked turbot with paper-thin crispy potatoes than a T-bone steak. This restaurant is the choice for seafood lovers who are exceptionally picky about freshness and sustainable fishing. You will pretty much be eating right across from where your food was sourced. It's worth each and every one of those twenty-three kilometers out of the center of Rome to get there.

What do you like most about living in Rome?

> *There are cities that can be circumnavigated within a known period of time, and you will have seen everything they have to offer. Rome's beauty and potential to amaze you repeatedly is simply boundless. That's why I can't live anywhere else.'*

Favorite Restaurant
— *Isola d'Oro*

My secret to happiness:

"Good health and world peace"

Alessasandro Scali

Jeweler

— Born and bred in Rome, recommends...

Made or Born Roman?

"Both of my parents and both sets of grandparents were born and raised in this city. I am extremely proud of this heritage."

🔒 Secret Spot
— *Trastevere's Tiny Alleys*

Not too secretive, but quite unique are the tiny roads around the Trastevere area. From an architectural point of view, what grabs your attention most are the terraces and balconies overlooking tiny alleys. I usually take long walks simply to enjoy the rich colors, textures, and even diverse sounds of silence.

🍷 Favorite Bar
— *Bar Gianicolo*

Piazzale Aurelio, 5

Finding bad coffee in Rome could be a laborious mission. But if you want more from your bar than caffeine, this bar will deliver a full-on Roman experience. The location is fantastic, with probably the most entertaining views in the world. A perfect place, even with kids, because while they run wild and free in the square, you can enjoy your coffee in peace.

🍴 Favorite Restaurant
—*Cave Canem*

Piazza di San Calisto, 11

Small, extremely welcoming, and off the tourist map. You'll find genuine Romans dining here, overlooking a bustling square. If the crunchy Roman pizza, perfect pasta, and homemade specialities like gorgonzola cheese-filled baked potatoes don't do it for you, the people-watching most certainly will.

What do you like most about living in Rome?

The amazing weather sets the scene here, and a good thing too, because much of Rome's beauty is outdoors. At the tender age of fifty, I find myself still discovering new places every day, and I think I will never exhaust all this city really has to offer."

Made or Born Roman?

> 66 *Born in Trastevere, in the heart of the city, and I've lived here ever since. That's what a real Roman is supposed to be like!"*

🔒 **Secret Spot**
— *Piazza San Cosimato*

At my ripe age, I seek a place that will keep me distracted, where I can meet my other retired friends, and this is the perfect spot. It's a square for all ages and tastes, surrounded by lots of bars, restaurants, churches. You have to be quite a special specimen if you end up feeling the tiniest bit bored here. We don't get too many tourists here, but the ones who do come are the ones in the know.

🍷 **Favorite Bar**
— *Giselda*

Viale Trastevere, 52

A modern bar that hasn't lost its tradition of good service. Their delicacies are all homemade and quite rich, but like all good things, moderation is recommended. Many groups of friends convene here, so if you go more than once, you will recognize familiar faces, and meet new ones. Unlike many places in Rome, you don't have to pay a premium to sit at the tables.

My secret to happiness:

"To remain optimistic, come what may"

Mario Luigi

⟨⟨⟨⟨⟨ **Retired Traffic Police Officer** ⟨⟨⟨⟨⟨

— Born and bred in Rome, recommends...

What do you like most about living in Rome?

> 66 *Let's face it, as far as modern European cities go, Rome can be dysfunctional in many ways.* **But it's the Romans and the proud history they herald that forces locals and visitors alike to overlook all that."**

 Favorite Restaurant
— *Ristorante al 34*

Via Mario de' Fiori, 34

Real Romans do not settle for a good plate of pasta; they aim for utter excellence. The pasta options at this restaurant are nothing short of incredible. It's a tiny place, so make sure you book a table, and the later the better, to avoid the early evening crowd, which tends to be rather noisy. You will be more relaxed when the noise level is down, which will allow you to savor the deliciousness they serve up disguised as mere food.

Favorite
Restaurant
— *Ristorante
Le Cave*

Made or Born Roman?

" *I was born and raised in Denmark but I met a Roman man in the summer of 1997 and a year later moved for love, just like the Woody Allen movie: To Rome with Love."*

What do you like most about living in Rome?

" *Being surrounded by beauty. The Roman sky is incredibly beautiful at any hour of the day. Living in Rome is like living in the middle of more than 2000 years of history. Even after having lived here for 18 years, Rome still takes my breath away."*

Susanne Bungaard

Opera Singer

— *Born in Denmark, based in Rome, recommends...*

🔒 Secret Spot
— *Villa Borghese*

An all-time favorite filled with breathtaking beautiful spots and views. I have always lived close by, but nowadays I mostly go there to run or meet friends for lunch at Casa del Cinema or at the beautiful café of the National Gallery of Modern and Contemporary Art. In the summer, it's perfect for delightful picnics and open-air free movies. Picturesque playgrounds and a charming zoo make it also ideal for kids.

🍷 Favorite Bar
— *Said - Antica Fabbrica del Cioccolato*

Via Tiburtina, 135

Located in the San Lorenzo area, this was an old chocolate factory transformed into a modern café and bistro. Great place to hang out during cold winter afternoons for a hot chocolate followed by an aperitif or dinner. I love the old chocolate machines, remnant from when it was a factory. Very cool shabby chic interiors. Delicious chocolate both to drink and eat.

🍴 Favorite Restaurant
—*Ristorante Le Cave (Da Sabatino)*

Piazza di Sant'Ignazio, 169

A family-run restaurant for fifty years. Sabatino was the father who founded the place, now run by his three daughters and son. Piazza Sant Ignazio is one of the most beautiful and scenic Baroque squares in Rome, and this is the only restaurant there. I have been dining there often since I moved to Rome. Parliament is nearby, so often you will run into celebrities or politicians. Well-prepared genuine Roman plates, don't miss out on the antipasti and traditional pasta like *bucatini all'amatriciana* or *pasta cacio e pepe*, and the fresh fish everyday.

St. Peter's Square,
Rome, 8.12 am

My secret to happiness:

"Unconditional serenity"

Flora

Happily Retired,

— *Born and based in Rome recommends...*

Made or Born Roman?

" *Born in this fine city, but would have also been quintessentially Roman by choice if I was born elsewhere."*

🔒 Secret Spot — *Campo de' Fiori*

I've traveled quite a bit around the world and noticed that most of the exciting destinations to visit are places where you do or see things. This square, like much of Rome, exudes pleasure simply by being within its orbit. You don't have to be doing much or seeing anything to feel alive while walking around there. I especially love Palazzo Farnese, where the French Embassy to Rome is located.

🍷 Favorite Bar — *Baylon Cafè*

Via di San Francesco a Ripa, 151

This is a popular bar in the hip and delightful neighborhood of Trastevere. In addition to outstanding coffee and pastries served buffet style, you'll find a wonderful selection of fresh juices. I often see foreign locals and students who come in for the free WiFi but end up staying for the chitchat, the chilled vibe, and the caffeine.

What do you like most about living in Rome?

" *Romans can be quite hard on themselves, but I'll go out on a limb and say that this city's charm is not only derived from its relics or its art, but its living, breathing citizens. Romans possess a wicked sense of humor, a stoic, wise perspective on life, and an unrivaled desire to party and have a good time."*

🍴 Favorite Restaurant — *Pianostrada*

Vicolo del Cedro, 26

This restaurant is run entirely by women—a mother, two daughters, and the token daughter-in-law, I think. The theme is rustic Roman food, with an elaborate street food twist. They use excellent, fresh ingredients and bake their own bread. My favorite dish is the cod burger. Terrific service.

Living Rome
— *Sublime beauty*

My secret to happiness:

"To live in the present"

Giancarlo Todaro

Engineer

— Born in Bari, now based in Rome, recommends...

Made or Born Roman?

> *Born in Bari in the region of Puglia, but I've been living in Rome for the last ten years. I originally moved here for college, but when I found a job I grabbed the opportunity and stayed, never looking back."*

🔒 Secret Spot
— Ponte Sisto

This Roman bridge manages to be the jack of all trades, and the master of all. If you want it to be romantic, it delivers. If you want it to be lively and euphoric with street musicians, it delivers. And if you want it to be a hiding place, it most certainly delivers, especially in the early hours of the day.

🍷 Favorite Bar
— Caffè San Cosimato

Piazza San Cosimato, 61

I am not sure if I come to Trastevere for this bar, or if I go to this bar for Trastevere. But that's inconsequential because I love them both equally. Many successful Roman bars tout lousy service as a sign of arrogance, but not here. They take care of their clients in the warmest way and think of small details like a piece of chocolate with your cappuccino that makes all the difference.

🍴 Favorite Restaurant
—La Matricianella

Via del Leone, 4

The signature dish here is fried fish, but I go there for their fried potato skins. For pasta lovers, the *bucatini cacio e pepe* is the sort of Roman dish that either makes or breaks your reputation. Needless to say, they nail it here. Portions are generous and prices are fair. If you want to risk not eating there, make sure you don't call in to reserve!

What do you like most about living in Rome?

> *This city is deliciously promiscuous. Everybody feels that she's theirs and theirs alone, when of course it serenades everyone who calls it home. I'm just thrilled to call this city mine. When you have totally run out of ideas of things to do, just step out and walk in the historic center for an instant happiness fix."*

Made or Born Roman?

> *Of seven Roman generations on my mother's side and three on my father's. I guess that makes me a pretty hard-core Roman."*

My secret to happiness:

"To remain eternally optimistic"

🔒 Secret Spot
— *Porta Portese*

This ancient city gate is located at the end of Via Portuense, close to the banks of the Tiber river in the southern edge of the Rione Trastevere area of Rome. History aside, the area is better known for a popular flea market held every Sunday. The joke, of course, is if your bike gets stolen on Saturday anywhere in Rome, you can always buy it back on Sunday at Porta Portese.

🍷 Favorite Bar
— *Bar d'Alfredo e Lia*

Via Giovanni Bettolo, 20

Romans are very exacting of their bars, and if one is unable to serve the coffee and pastries just right, they move on to the next. I am exceptionally loyal to this bar because it reminds me of my youth. The owner is like an uncle to me and we're on a first-name basis. My loyalty is well rewarded because the coffee is incredible and the pastries and panini are out of this world.

Stefano d'Orazio

Businessman

— *Born in northern Italy, now based in Rome, recommends...*

What do you like most about living in Rome?

> *Jovial, mature citizens, perfect weather, and a beautiful city are the three elements that are hard to replicate in one place. I have traveled a lot and I concluded that Rome is the most 'liveable' of all major cities."*

🍴 Favorite Restaurant
— *Osteria degli Ubertini*

Via Guglielmo degli Ubertini, 77

My criteria for a great restaurant is to eat well at fair prices. This place ticks both boxes, and more. Few tourists know of this place, which is a great sign. Homey and attentive service sets them apart from most Roman restaurants. The food is amazing, especially their typical Roman dishes. Go for their soups in winter, and the *gnocchi al ragù* pretty much any time of the year.

Favorite
Restaurant
— *Otello alla*
Concordia

🔒 Secret Spot
— *Piazza di Pietra*

I come here to stay in touch with my inner passion for art. Here you will find the famous temple of Hadrian, built by his adoptive son and successor Antoninus Piusas, as a gift for his sister and to women. He used to claim that this is the spot that most revealed women's spirituality. Indeed, being an artist dedicated to divulging the strength of women in providing dignity and not just pleasure, I feel energized in this square.

🍷 Favorite Bar
— *Bar Salotto 42*

Piazza di Pietra, 42

The walls of this bar are adorned with art books, so naturally this is where I feel most at home. If you are familiar with Italian pop culture, you'll be pleasantly surprised to run into well-known actors, some of whom may even be starring in contemporary hits. Even the waiters, all astonishingly good looking, are themselves aspiring actors.

Fabiana Roscioli

Artist

— Born and raised in Rome, recommends...

My secret to happiness:

"To love my inner-self"

Made or Born Roman?

❝ *Born and raised in Rome, but I've never taken this privilege for granted. Grateful to call this magnificent place my town."*

What do you like most about living in Rome?

❝ *I am a fountain-lover, and Rome has some of the most stunning fountains in the world. Many are not that famous, but still carry rich history. I also love the taste of water in Rome, and watching the sun setting on ruins and bridges."*

🍴 Favorite Restaurant
—*Otello alla Concordia*

Via della Croce, 81

I come from a family of artists and this restaurant has been a hub for artistic souls for decades now. Strategically located near the Spanish steps, famous film producers, actors, Roman nobility, and politicians all dine here for their excellent Roman fare and rich wine selection.

My secret to happiness:

"To be able to enjoy the sound of silence"

Giuliana Scalmani

Business Owner

— Born and raised in Rome, recommends...

Made or Born Roman?

> *Born and raised in one of the oldest neighborhoods of ancient Rome, San Lorenzo, which was totally razed during the Second World War. To date, under the Basilica of San Lorenzo, there are bombs yet to be dismantled."*

🔒 Secret Spot
— *Basilica of San Clemente al Laterano*

I am passionate about the 'secret' layers of Rome. This city was built on three layers, which is best viewed at the Basilica of San Clemente al Laterano. Go down one flight of stairs, and you will find another Christian basilica from the fourth century with incredibly well-preserved frescoes. If you descend another flight of stairs you will come across a wealthy man's house from the first century.

🍷 Favorite Bar
— *Il Piccolo*

Via del Governo Vecchio, 74

If you want to get a glimpse of where hard-core Romans go for coffee, you won't find a better place. Come here to feel at home. You may even find some locals in their slippers down for a takeaway croissant. But don't let the casual vibe here mislead you into believing that this place is anything less than serious about the quality of their coffee.

🍴 Favorite Restaurant
— *Osteria Jenny*

Piazza dei Campani, 14/15

My kitchen is the best place to eat in Rome, but failing that, Osteria Jenny is a worthy second. I won't waste your time telling you how good the pasta is, how succulent the meat is, or how traditional and unpretentious this place is. All I have to say is that this is probably the only place I know that will cook your own snails if you bring them with you, the traditional Roman way.

What do you like most about living in Rome?

> *One of Rome's biggest conundrums, and perhaps its most charming feature, is that you will never be able to change it. This is a city that has to be lived by the day and instead of trying hard to change it, be open to be changed by it. Because you will be all the better for it."*

Made or Born Roman?

> *Born in Rome to a Roman mother and a semi-Roman father, from a small town on the outskirts of the city called Acquafondata.*"

Secret Spot
— *Ponte Galeria*

Slightly outside of Rome, this is an amazing spot worth visiting. It's at the end of the airplane landing runways at Fiumicino airport. Even if you aren't an aviation fanatic as I am, nothing beats lying down on the soft grass, observing gigantic jetliners hovering over your face and landing mere meters away from you.

Favorite Bar
— *Il Caffè*

Via Leonori Aristide, 91

This bar is celebrated for its choice of superb coffee beans. I should know—I used to own the place at one point, but sold it to open a bigger bar in a different location. That said, I still give a huge big thumbs up to the new owners because they took what we started and improved on it. It's one of the best bars in town.

Roberto Renzi

Businessman

— *Born on the outskirts of Rome, recommends...*

What do you like most about living in Rome?

> *Rome feels like a village that's pretending to be a real city. If you are a real local, chances are you will feel that everywhere you go you* meet someone you know, let alone in the areas that you frequent regularly. This feeling of belonging grounds me and makes me appreciate this city.*"

Favorite Restaurant
— *Casa Bleve*

Via del Teatro Valle, 48

Not cheap, but definitely worth a visit. Close to many must-visit spots in Rome, this place offers amazing Roman dishes and excellent wine options, especially red. The service is impeccable. From the moment you step in until you leave, you'll feel pampered, but not in the cheesy over-the-top way. Run by a pretty large family of grandparents, mothers, fathers, sons, daughters, uncles—you get the picture. If they like you, they may even take you on a tour of their wine cellars. Without googling what it means, order *guancia di manzo al Barolo*. Trust me.

Made or Born Roman?

I was born and raised in this city, but feel that my identity is not enshrined by that birthright, as much as I had to earn the right to be a genuine Roman of my own accord."

My secret to happiness:

"To have the perfect partner by my side"

Silvia Persi

Graphic Designer

— *Born and raised in Rome, recommends...*

🔒 Secret Spot
— *Piazza della Minerva*

Rome has numerous secret spots to hide and be left alone with one's thoughts. This is my favorite one where I sit on the stairway to the church and observe people while enjoying a tasty crushed coffee ice cream that you can buy at the nearby bar La Tazza D'oro.

🍷 Favorite Bar
— *Panella*
Via Merulana, 54

Breakfast for me is the most important meal of the day, and I eat a lot. But when I like to splurge a little and spoil myself with a tasty coffee surrounded by some of the finest specimens of good-looking people, I go to this bar in the new part of Rome. I almost feel young again! Hefty bill aside, their pastries and coffee are really good as is the lunch buffet.

🍴 Favorite Restaurant
— *Ristorante Ai Piani*
Via Francesco Denza, 35

Primarily a seafood restaurant run by a second-generation family from Sardegna. Let the owner choose your meal and trust you will be fed well. The price-to-quality ratio is excellent. Their wine list is spectacular and trust their recommendations of pairing wine to food. They never try to upsell you expensive wine. When you leave, you will not know what hit you the most, the culinary heaven they serve, or the warmth of spirit and hospitality.

What do you like most about living in Rome?

I am in love with the hidden and the unknown that characterizes Rome. At first glance, you may be under the illusion that you can conquer Rome and see everything it has to offer. Even locals who've spent a lifetime here will never really run this city's course. Couple that with the perfect climate, and you really get the perfect city.

My secret to happiness:

"To watch my children growing up"

Carlo Parisella

Personal Trainer

— *Born and based in Rome, recommends...*

Made or Born Roman?

❝ *Full-blooded Roman, of at least two generations. My grandfather was born here in 1886, and we've been here since.* ❞

🔒 **Secret Spot**
— *Circus Maximus*

For a health and fitness enthusiast like me, I absolutely love the outdoors. There is no better outdoor space to go for a run or a workout than Circus Maximus, an ancient Roman chariot racing stadium and mass entertainment venue. You will feel like a Roman gladiator, updated for our times.

🏆 **Favorite Bar**
— *Nik Bar*

Largo Somalia, 51

I am a big fan of the simple Italian breakfast: cappuccino and *cornetto*. This bar is renowned for its creamy cappuccinos, with a sprinkle of cocoa powder. Their pastries are also certifiably delicious, crunchy on the outside and gooey in the middle. But because they are not too rich, I never catch myself calorie counting.

🍴 **Favorite Restaurant**
— *Due Ladroni*

Piazza Nicosia, 24

This is a restaurant for all tastes, but their culinary genius shines through seafood. Their ingredients are fresh and top quality. I eat there often. There is something about the way they marinate fish, cook it, and serve it up to you that leaves you speechless after the first bite. I often hesitate before digging into the plate to avoid ruining the picture-perfect presentation. Add to that impeccable and fast service.

What do you like most about living in Rome?

❝ *I think that's an unfair question to ask, because a city like Rome is loveable for myriad reasons. I can't pinpoint one clear one, but what I do know is that despite all of its challenges, I can never imagine myself living anywhere else. And that's not due to any lack of imagination on my part!* ❞

🔒 Secret Spot
— *The sea*

This will sound like I am copping out in my response, but my secret spot is to take my boat out to sea. Many people who visit Rome really have no idea how close the city is to the seaside, and that there is an active beach and boating culture. You can charter a boat for a day or a week and visit some of the smaller islands within a day's sail from Rome. Totally breathtaking.

🍷 Favorite Bar
— *I Siciliani*
Viale Europa, 134

The vast majority of bars in Rome know what they are doing when it comes to coffee. I am not picky, but I am partial to this one bar in the new part of Rome, EUR. As a pilot, I often stop there early in the mornings for a coffee ahead of a flight, and am often tempted by some of their Sicilian delicacies. And it's much more than cannoli.

My secret to happiness:

"To be in harmony with the world"

Made or Born Roman?

> *If they had sniffer dogs to detect Romans, they would sniff me out hundreds of miles away. I'm as Roman as you can get."*

Roberto Oppizio

Commercial Pilot

— *Born and raised in Rome, recommends...*

What do you like most about living in Rome?

> *I've visited numerous cities across the world, and not just as a fleeting pilot who only gets a superficial sense of a place. Rome is hands down the most beautiful city in the world despite whatever flaws it may have."*

Favorite Restaurant
— *Da Romolo al Porto*

Via Porto Innocenziano, 19, Anzio

This is a small restaurant located in the seaside city of Anzio, within a short driving distance from Rome. You can either eat indoors or by the sea. They prepare and serve seafood in a unique way. You start with more than thirty raw and cooked seafood appetizers, then move on to the entrees. The raw appetizers will make the best sushi you've ever had seem so bland. Drinks are included and you pretty much stop eating when you've had enough, all for one set price. They own their own fishing boat, so what you eat is what they caught.

**Favorite
Restaurant**
— *Osteria Gildo il
Cacciatore*

Made or Born Roman?

> *I was born in Ancona, but when my father got a job here in 1949, we all moved with him.*

🔒 **Secret Spot**
— *The Observatory at Monte Mario*

This is one of the most significant heritages of the city, and it deserves the same attention that some of the other more popular tourist destinations garner. And I don't mean just for its spectacular views, but because of the breadth of cultural and historic wealth one can experience visiting it. Plan to spend a full day there to enjoy it most.

🍷 **Favorite Bar**
— *Vanni*

Via Col di Lana, 10

Do they make spectacular coffee and delicious pastries? Absolutely. But that's not why I love this bar. I go for the vibe. The clientele there are more mature, successful adults rather than rambunctious youths. If you are feeling decadent, order their Maritozzi—a Roman pastry that resembles a doughnut but with a unique, creamy filling.

Emidio Vitaletti

Retired

— *Born in Ancona, now lives in Rome, recommends...*

My secret to happiness:

"To be fair and loyal to others"

What do you like most about living in Rome?

> *After living in a city for this long, it is only natural that you are more aware of what you least like, rather than what you appreciate most. In my case, the noise and growing pollution in the busiest parts weighs on my mind. But this pales in comparison with why I never left this city.*

🍴 **Favorite Restaurant**
—*Osteria Gildo il Cacciatore*

Via di Boccea, 348

This is a solid, traditional eatery that gets meat, fish, and pizza exceptionally right. I am a bit of a traditionalist when it comes to food, so my favorite dish there is a Roman classic, bucatini pasta with amatricciana sauce. If you go there with a healthy appetite, start with their fried appetizers—*Fiori di Zucca, Olive Ascolane,* and *Il Baccalà.* No matter how much you eat, wind it all down with the happiest of endings—the crema catalane dessert.

"*I love the reflection of the light and the monuments on the river, and the salmon and golden sunsets.*"

GRAZIA DEL GIUDICE, PAGE 24

Gianicolo, 5.12 pm

My secret to happiness:

"To absorb the happiness surrounding me"

Francesco Mossa

Architect

— *Born and raised in Rome, recommends...*

Favorite Restaurant
— *MeAt*

Via Portuense, 465

Don't let the name deceive you. This is not a temple for carnivores, but a typical Roman eatery with a uniquely friendly vibe, shockingly good service, and fair prices. I'd say stick to the Roman classics on the menu, and don't take a risk with what may seem experimental on paper. I've had the best *pasta cacio e pepe* there.

Secret Spot
— *Villa Celimontana*

This villa on the Caelian Hill in Rome is best known for its gardens, but if you happen to be a fan of jazz or music in general, this is the spot for you. Great for kids, and the perfect spot to chill out, relax, or spend a fun afternoon with drink in hand. The ambience is incredible, and if you are lucky, you may catch some of the biggest names in jazz playing here. Summer is when the A-listers show up.

Favorite Bar
— *Il Maritozzaro*

Via Ettore Rolli, 50

This is one of the oldest bars in town and they serve the best *maritozzo* in Rome. A *maritozzo* is essentially a sweet roll filled to the brim with fresh whipped cream, typical of the Lazio region. Needless to say, they get their coffee superbly right, too.

What do you like most about living in Rome?

When you look beneath the surface of Rome as a top tourist destination with outstanding architectural beauty, it's a tough city to navigate. But Romans are equally as resilient and they have learned to adapt with whatever comes their way. This indomitable spirit is what I love most about living here, as I feel it has rubbed off on me.

Made or Born Roman?

It may be clear from my Roman accent. Born and raised in Rome.

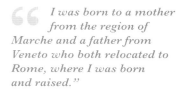

Made or Born Roman?

My secret to happiness:

"To dream, but also be content with what I have"

Stefano Castro

Economist

— *Born and raised in Rome, recommends...*

🔒 Secret Spot
— *Anzio*

One of Rome's beauties is that it is close to both the mountains and sea. My secret spot is the latter. Anzio is a seaside town just south of Rome. Whenever I have any free time for myself, I escape there. Rome's beaches are more spectacular during the winter season when the ambience is calmer and more romantic. A delicious glass of wine in hand, finger food to nibble on, and the wide open sea ahead make it just perfect.

🍷 Favorite Bar
— *Danieli Pasticceria E Caffè*

Viale Regina Margherita, 209

Excellent, attentive service despite the thick throng of crowds who frequent this bar. Here you will find an endless array of delicious house specialties like their to-die-for pistachio *cornetti*. But be smart and go for the mini-sized *cornetti* to feel less bloated and to try more than one flavor. Needless to say, they don't just make coffee here, they worship it.

🍴 Favorite Restaurant
—*Orlando*

Via Sicilia, 41

This is run by a Sicilian family and it's become my go-to place whenever I crave seafood. Even when I need to take out someone for a business lunch, I always end up there. Here you will find fresh, amazing tasting fare with highly original presentation. Their mantra is to delight their guests, so there are numerous house favorites that you can really only find there. The fried squid is nothing short of addictive.

What do you like most about living in Rome?

I love that it's a city that allows you to wake up and stroll into its historic center while everyone else is still lazy at home or sleeping. Like two passionate lovers, Rome will likely seduce you in private and fool you into believing she's just all yours."

Made or Born Roman?

> 66 *I moved to Rome eight years ago from the north, because I fell in love with a Roman and wanted to work in a pediatric hospital there.*"

🔒 Secret Spot
— *Villa Pamphili*

When I am yearning for some tranquility and downtime, my first port of call is Villa Pamphili despite it being quite expansive and highly public. There are a few nooks and crannies that are still unknown to the populous at large where you can hide and become invisible for a while. If you like outdoor sports, this is also the most ideal location for that.

🍷 Favorite Bar
— *Caffetteria Italia*
Piazza Venezia

During any season, this bar is blessed with one of the best views in the world. It's inside the Vittorio Emanuele II Monument. For most Romans, coffee drinking is like worship, so it's even better when the temple is so beautiful. My favorite coffee drink is the cappuccino because it takes longer to sip than a coffee, but is not as milky as a caffè latte.

My secret to happiness:

"To do what you love most, day in, day out, relentlessly"

Francesca Bassani

Pediatrician

— *Born in the north, adopted by Rome, recommends...*

What do you like most about living in Rome?

> 66 *I could tell you the history, the culture, and the art, and I wouldn't be lying. I love these things. But for me, the main pull factor here is to know that every day you can discover something new. Actually, I take that back, not 'can discover' but "will discover.' It's inevitable in Rome.*"

🍴 Favorite Restaurant
—*Il Miraggio*
Via della Lungara, 16

Everything that defines real Romans is exemplified in this restaurant. The spaghetti *alle vongole veraci* (wild clams) is a signature dish here. The *carciofi fritti* (fried artichokes) for an appetizer sounds a lot more evil than it really is. Yes it's fried, but it's not oily or overpowering. Originally a Roman Jewish delicacy, this has now become a symbol of all Roman cuisine. It's perfectly crispy and absolutely addictive. The delicious food aside, you will also fall in love with the location of this restaurant, surrounded by lush botanical gardens.

Favorite Bar
— *Il Pozzo del Gelato*

Made or Born Roman?

> *I was born and raised in Rome. I think unlike other people, Romans take their identity to heart. They live and breathe it, rather than just throw it about like an empty title.*

 **Secret Spot**
— *Fregene*

One of Rome's best-kept secrets is its proximity to the seaside. Most visitors to the city only flock to the historic center and never venture to the lakes or the sea. This small seaside town is where I love to go to relax. It's never more than a thirty-minute drive, but once you are there, you forget completely the business of Rome, and bask in the tranquility of Mediterranean beach life.

 **Favorite Bar**
— *Il Pozzo del Gelato*
Viale Isacco Newton, 84

Like all self-respecting Romans, I am in a committed relationship with my local bar, but I also cheat on it occasionally with this joint. Coffee and pastries aside, which they do really well, this is a great place for a delicious homemade gelato or a chilled-out apertif in the evening with yummy finger food for a set price.

Stefania Carfora

Stylist

— *Born and raised in Rome, recommends...*

What do you like most about living in Rome?

> *I like that Rome is small and you can walk to a different area in under ten minutes. I like the craziness of Rome,*

I enjoy the hustle and bustle of the people. People pay good money to go to far places to see beauty, but all I need to do is step outside."

 Favorite Restaurant
— *Il gECOBIOndo*
Via Gerolamo Cardano, 105

While Rome has a rich culinary heritage, until recently it's been quite difficult to find good vegan or vegetarian restaurants. But this is slowly starting to change. This restaurant is one of my favorite vegan joints, although it is small and cozy, with a homey feel to it. The real star is the food. Exciting vegan takes on classic Italian dishes like lasagna that will leave you salivating for more.

My secret to happiness:

"My family, my husband, and my children"

Alessia Cerilli

Employee

— Born and raised in Rome, recommends...

Made or Born Roman?

> *Not only was I born and raised in Rome, but I grew up in a neighborhood just a short walking distance from the Vatican."*

What do you like most about living in Rome?

> *I don't think I've ever stopped to ponder what it is I like most about Rome. It's a love affair. You never analyze what it is you love most about your lover. It's a package."*

🍴 Favorite Restaurant
— *Pizza Ciro*

Via della Mercede, 43, Rome

Like the delicious Neapolitan cuisine that this restaurant specializes in, a friendly atmosphere is very much at hand there. I come here for the traditional Neapolitan pizza crust—thick and juicy, not like the paper-thin and crusty Roman variety that I am not particularly fond of. Their house wine is delicious by any standard.

🍷 Favorite Bar
— *Nik Bar*

Viale Somalia, 51

This bar has been standing proudly and serving our community since 1969. Like any bar in Rome, if you make yourself a regular, your every wish will be granted. Great-tasting coffee and, hands down, the best *cornetti* in Europe. The other pastries are addictively delicious too.

🔒 Secret Spot
— *St. Peter's Square*

I grew up near the Vatican, so the way I relate to it is very different from how most tourists perceive this iconic square. I met the love of my life there, so for me it's more than just a pretty part of Rome with religious connotations, but one that underpins the very essence and joy of life.

Made or Born Roman?

> *I was born in Rome to an Italian father and a Peruvian mother. A small part of me is Latin American, but the rest is Roman to the bone."*

🔒 Secret Spot
— *Ponte Sant'Angelo*

This is a breathtaking bridge connecting the city center of Rome to the towering Castel Sant'Angelo. It spans the Tiber river with five arches. No cars are permitted so it's pedestrian heaven with dramatic views on both sides. It's also a stone's throw from the Vatican on one side, and Villa Borghese on the other end.

🍷 Favorite Bar
— *Caffè Perù*

Via di Monserrato, 46, Roma

No matter where other Romans tell you to go to get the best coffee in town, I guarantee you this bar is better. Many bars claims they make delicious cappuccinos, and that may very well be true, but at this place, they've got it down to a science. And they share the love, they tell you all their trade secrets. Like the secret to make the perfect cappuccino is never to allow the milk to boil over twice.

My secret to happiness:

"To fall in love unconditionally"

Francesca

Beautician

— *Born and raised in Rome, recommends...*

What do you like most about living in Rome?

> *I love that change is very gradual and sluggish in Rome. There are no drastic sharp turns or unexpected shifts, which for someone like me, who likes to live life at a leisurely tempo, is just perfect."*

🍴 Favorite Restaurant
— *Mamutones*

Piazza Monte Gennaro, 29

This is a humble joint in the north of Rome, but still my favorite restaurant in town because I feel at home there. I love the coziness of this place and the warmth and attentiveness of the owners. The *maltagliati, ceci, cozze e vongole* is by far my favorite dish there.

My secret to happiness:

"My two sons"

Simona Falso

EU Parliament Officer

— Grew up in Avellino, born and based in Rome, recommends...

Made or Born Roman?

Secret Spot
— Tiber Bridges

Every single one of these bridges crisscrossing the river Tiber carries a plethora of secrets, history, and indescribable charm. The sort of feelings they invoke can't be expressed in words, but have to be felt. In summer when the weather is gorgeous, I like to stroll from one bank to the other to lose myself.

Favorite Bar
— Bar Quattro Venti Caffè

Viale dei Quattro Venti, 102

The sun always shines on this bar. By the time I am out of the door and I'm ready to start my day with a cappuccino and *cornetto*, my favorite bar is always basking in honey-hued sunrays. They know me by name and unless I am in the mood for something else, my order is ready by the time I get to the counter, without saying a single word other than good morning to my superhero baristas.

Favorite Restaurant
—Teorema di Euclide

Piazza Euclide, 45

This is one of the oldest locales in town, and until recently the regulars just called it 'the old joint.' More recently, it's been taken over by a younger group of investors who've turned it around in a spectacular way that maintained the old charm, including a chef from Puglia who's famed for always surprising his patrons with signature dishes from his region.

What do you like most about living in Rome?

Rome is the sort of city where anything, even that which is beyond your wildest imagination, can happen. Yet, at the same time, the warmth of the city emanates from its familiarity and predictability. You can go to places where you'll see familiar faces, or you can escape and become incognito for as long as you need to."

My secret to happiness:

"Discover new people and cultures through traveling"

Ida D'Alessandro

Marketing and Communication Expert

— Based in Rome, recommends...

🍴 Favorite Restaurant
—*Roma Sparita*

Piazza di Santa Cecilia, 24

In the vibrant neighborhood of Trastevere, this place overlooks the delectable Piazza di Santa Cecilia. A tiny family-owned restaurant that keeps it pure and simple by offering traditional Roman dishes done right. To enjoy it most, eat there when it's not too hot and not too crowded so you can sit outside. I recommend the *tonnarelli cacio e pepe* served on a crusty bed of delicious parmesan cheese.

Made or Born Roman?

❝ *I was born in a tiny village on the outskirts of Rome, but my family moved to the city, where I grew up.*❞

🔒 Secret Spot
— *Basilica di Santa Sabina*

This is one of the oldest churches in Rome, perched on the majestic Aventino Hill. I go there to bask in the silence of its Roman cloister, admire its astonishing mosaics, and escape the hustle and bustle of the eternal city. It's a short walk away from Il Giardino degli Aranci, which is a perfect spot to enjoy one of the most beautiful views of Rome from the garden's terrace.

What do you like most about living in Rome?

❝ *Rome always surprises me. There is a glimpse of eternity tucked in the most unexpected places. I adore the sunsets from the Gianicolo terrace, the noise of the market in Campo de' Fiori, the silence of its churches and cloisters, and the magnificence of its monuments. Sometimes I wish I was born elsewhere to discover the eternal city with fresh eyes every day.*❞

🍷 Favorite Bar
— *ViVi Bistrot*

Villa Doria Pamphili, Via Vitellia, 102

Located in one of the most beautiful green spaces in Rome, this bar has an unfair location advantage. But it's not one of those touristic joints that rests on its laurels. Magical location aside, they serve a wonderful breakfast. I go there to enjoy a perfect espresso and homemade cakes, sitting outside immersing myself in this wondrous location wrapped in the simplicity of nature.

Made or Born Roman?

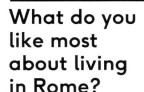

> *Born and raised in Rome. I won't lie, there are times when I flirt with the idea of moving somewhere else, but the fact that I'm still hear speaks volumes for the city's magnetic pull factor."*

What do you like most about living in Rome?

> *I love seeing swarms of tourists everywhere, knowing they are coming to my city. The notion that all these diverse people from around the world have convened here to see something special makes me feel proud, as well as grateful."*

My secret to happiness:
"Finding your inner peace, and taming your inner demons"

🔒 Secret Spot
— *Parco Centrale del Lago*

Many people feel the historic part of Rome defines the city. I do not disagree, but I also love some of Rome's more modern quarters. The lake in the EUR neighbourhood of Rome is one of the most serene parts of the city where I love to take my dog for a walk, rest under to take a nap or read, before crossing the street for a stiff coffee at one of the many bars in the area.

💡 Favorite Bar
— *Caffè Palombini*

Piazzale Konrad Adenauer, 12

In the heart of Mussolini's urban project, Eur, this bar is something of an institution. It's extremely spacious, unlike most Roman bars. Everything here is overpriced, so you are paying for the privilege of hanging out with some of Rome's most beautiful and successful citizens. Free WiFi and if the name sounds familiar, that is because they also supply their hugely successful coffee brand to other bars.

Chiara Innocenzi
Student

— Born and raised in Rome, recommends...

🍴 Favorite Restaurant
—*Fish Market*

Vicolo della Luce, 2

This small, hole-in-the-wall restaurant evolved from a tiny fishmonger in Trastevere. But from these humble roots rose a hip, successful seafood joint with a twist. You tick what you want to eat on a sheet of paper and take it to the kitchen to wait while it is prepared. This is fun and minimizes the possibility of bad service. Be prepared to wait in line during peak hours. The fish burger and the tuna tartar are essential things to order.

Favorite
Restaurant
— *Ristorante Cesar,*
La Posta Vecchia
Hotel

Made or Born Roman?

> *I was born and raised in Rome, and have experienced the city both as a young single professional and a working mother."*

What do you like most about living in Rome?

> *I grew up here thinking of Rome as a nightmare city: crazy traffic, tardiness, ill-preparedness for rain. But the more you live here, the better prepared you are to look above Rome's chaos to see the inherent beauty of city. I take public transport and walk, which is the easiest way to be seduced by Rome. Is it a challenging city? Sure. But the art, history, and architecture feed your soul and make up for everything else."*

My secret to happiness:

"To surround myself with positive energy"

Giovanna Todini

Marketing Consultant

— Born and raised in Rome, recommends...

Favorite Bar
— Le Café Vert

Via Anton Giulio Barrili, 47

In the heart of Gianicolo, above Trastevere where I live, this is my go-to day-to-day bar. The coffee is always perfect, always a hit, never a miss. Their homemade tarts and pies are delicious. The background music is excellent and not invasive, and the free WiFi means I can also get some work done.

Secret Spot
— Basilica di Santa Maria Maggiore

In a city with nearly one thousand churches brimming with frescoes, sculptures, and the genius art of Bernini, Borromini, and Caravaggio, it's hard to pick a favorite, but this Basilica designed by Michelangelo comes close. Every Sunday at precisely 11:20 a.m., don't miss the breathtaking music from a stunning organ made of cherry and walnut wood. The instrument was bequeathed to the church by Pope Giovanni Paolo II.

Favorite Restaurant
— Ristorante Cesar, La Posta Vecchia Hotel

Strada Ciclabile Palo Laziale, Ladispoli

For a romantic, elegant but informal lunch or dinner during spring and summer, this place is slightly out of Rome on the coast, but well worth the trip. With a well-deserved Michelin star, go there for traditional Italian fare with a sophisticated, contemporary twist. Fresh produce is sourced from their own organic garden. Savor the best Mediterranean dishes with the soft sound of waves in the background against the most beautiful sunset.

An interview with

Carmine Manduca
Barista

Carmine Manduca is a Roman barista working at a popular coffee bar in the EUR neighborhood.

How did you become a barista?

Dumb luck. Fifteen years ago, I was a waiter at a resort in my home region of Calabria. The hotshot barista at that joint injured himself and was unable to work one day. And who did they ask to step in? Me. I fell in love with the job, and the life that comes with it, within about thirty seconds of making and serving my first espresso. I have never looked back.

What makes for great coffee, theory or practice?

Understanding the coffee bean is essential. How to toast, store, grind, handle, and brew it. How to love it, really. If the raw material is less than perfect, no amount of wizardry at the bar can make good coffee out of bad. When you respect the coffee bean, it rewards you with sublime coffee, consistently. And that's the secret of this business, how to be consistent.

And the role of the barista?

No two baristas are alike, but there are some fundamentals we all respect. Above all, to pour coffee in a hot cup. That alone makes a huge difference. If you are mixing in milk, like a caffè latte, the milk needs to be mounted at the right temperature, never exceeding seventy degrees °C (158 °F), or you risk the milk caramelizing or over-foaming. And of course, the cardinal rules of rations between coffee and milk depending on the drink.

How about working with low-fat dairy milk or even alternative milks like soy, rice, and almond?

Each variant requires a totally different procedure. Full cream milk is the easiest to work with, period. Still, we must keep learning to keep up with the changing tastes of our customers, their dietary requirements, their allergies and intolerances. Ten years ago, the purists amongst us rebuffed these alternative milk types as 'un-Italian,' and some still do. I call that arrogance. As a barista, my main imperative is that everyone enjoys their breakfast at the bar, not to pass judgement or to appoint myself as the coffee police.

What do you prefer, being behind the coffee machine (machinista), or at the bar taking orders (barista)?

Both are demanding as hell. I have a slight preference of working the machine because you see the satisfaction on your client's face the minute they take the first sip. Still, it's also fun to interact with people, especially the regulars. Both jobs

> **I fell in love with the job, and the life that comes with it, within about thirty seconds of making and serving my first espresso.**

require a solid memory, and the roles are interdependent. If the chemistry between the barista and machinista is less than stellar, all hell can break loose. And you wouldn't want that to happen at peak hour because you risk being lynched.

Foreigners are rather amused by the vast number of coffee variations available in Italy. Please set the record straight. Exactly how many are there?
Honestly, who's to say? My unscientific guess is more than fifty, but people are always coming up with new ones. And if they can dream it, we can make it, and if we can make it once, it's official.

What is the rarest request you've ever gotten?
Cold ginseng cappucino with soy milk. And may I never get it again.

Now come clean. How many coffees do you drink per day?
Five or six. Maybe seven. Sometimes eight, okay? With breakfast I have two or three, and the rest throughout the day.

What are the hours like?
Mornings are brutal. We open up and start prepping at the crack of dawn. Our witching hour is 8:30 a.m. and it lasts until 10:30. We pick up again after lunch, but it's mostly straight espressos rather than all the fun, exotic requests we get in the morning.

How about tourists who stumble in asking for, God forbid, filter coffee?
We don't discriminate. Personally, I cringe at the thought of filtered coffee, because it's simply not what coffee is about. But who am I to superimpose my personal likes and dislikes on others? If someone comes in and asks for an 'Americano,' I'll prepare it and serve it in the best possible way I know. That said, most tourists, Americans included, come with an open mind and an eagerness to try our traditional Italian coffees. ▮▮

An interview with

Simone Strano
Photographer

More than the rest of us, photographers have a rare gift of perceiving life from a slightly more interesting, slightly more evocative angle. Which means their interpretation of a city so frequently photographed like Rome can be illuminating.

Simone Strano is a successful photographer who lives and works in Rome. He moved to the city from his native Naples in 2002 for a photography course, but never went back.

What makes Rome so photogenic?

The history, pervading every inch of this town. Wherever you look around you will see history and culture where you expect to see them and where you least expect to come across them. Even in the supposedly modern quarters of Rome, you will still find ancient walls, stones, sculptures, paintings, and ruins. And to top it all, this amazing subject matter is presented under a unique Roman light, this honey-amber tinged hue that is virtually impossible to find elsewhere in the world. Just like the smells and sounds, every city has its unique light DNA, and Rome's just happens to be particularly beautiful.

Can a city be over-photographed?

Yes. Every city, including Rome, has no dearth of cheesy, repetitive, clichéd images that are hashed and rehashed. It's what photographers loathe the most. In Rome, the image of the overweight centurions and gladiators posing for the camera by the Pantheon or Colosseum is the gold standard in bad taste. If cringing could kill, I'd be long dead.

Has the advent of mobile phones with mega-powerful cameras contributed to this overexposure of cities?

I love the endless possibilities mobile cameras present for photography. In a way, they don't just democratize photography, but they also liberate it and take it to places we could only dream of in the past. Even professional photographers don't always strut around with their high-end cameras and lenses. When you live in a city like Rome, brimming with amazing photo adventures and opportunities, the portability of a very decent camera makes all the difference. I firmly believe that great photography has nothing to do with technology, as much as it's a factor of a keen aesthetic sense and an eye for beauty. You need to be able to recognize what's beautiful before you can capture it. Increasingly, there are some very talented photographers who have decided to only work with mobile cameras as their primary

> **Even professional photographers don't always strut around with their high-end cameras and lenses.**

tool, with outstanding results. On the other hand, I absolutely despise the culture of selfies, and if I could, I would legislate to ban those damn selfie sticks. When I see tourists and visitors to Rome lost and self-absorbed in the selfie 'oblivion' as I call it, snapping mediocre pictures of themselves doing ridiculous things like pouting or flashing a victory sign, right by some of the most important and historic landmarks known to human civilization, it really ticks me off. They are depriving themselves of living the moment and enjoying the space they are in, while at the same time polluting the virtual airwaves with even more mindless digital fluff.

Where would you advise visitors to Rome to take rare, interesting, or beautiful photos that veer away from the iconic or stereotypical ones?
One of my favorite spots that's largely off the beaten track is Aventino Hill. Not many tourists flock there of their own devices, although as an area, it's chockfull of incredible corners, hidden visual gems, amazing gardens, and breathtaking churches.

Another well-kept secret is Via Giulia, adjacent to the noisy and super-crowded Campo de' Fiori, but unexpectedly serene and quiet. It's a treasure trove of indescribably beautiful buildings, ornate architectural details, timeless history, and incredible courtyards. It's as close as you could get to a time machine that swiftly transports you back to a different period, in this case, ancient Rome.

Directory

Restaurants

Quick Dining Glossary

Acqua frizzante: sparkling water
Acqua liscia: still water
Al dente: firm (pasta)
Al sangue: rare (meat)
Antipasto: appetizer
Ben cotta: well done (meat)
Biologico: organic
Cena: dinner
Colazione: breakfast
Cottura media: medium (meat)
Di stagione: in season
Il conto: the check
Pane: bread
Piatto del giorno: dish of the day
Piccante: spicy
Pranzo: lunch
Senza glutine: gluten free
Senza lattosio: dairy free
Un bicchiere d'acqua: a glass of water
Vino della casa: house wine

Bars

Quick Bar Glossary

Aperitivo: the ritual of going out for a pre-dinner drink and light snacks

Caffè: espresso

Caffè decaffeinato: decaf espresso

Caffè in vetro: espresso in a glass

Caffè corto: short, intense espresso

Caffè lungo: long espresso (more water)

Caffè macchiato: espresso 'stained' with milk foam

Caffè Corretto: espresso, 'corrected' with a shot of alcohol, usually grappa

Caffè Americano: espresso in a tall glass with 60% water, mimicking American filtered coffee

Caffè latte: espresso and steamed milk

Caffè napoletano: espresso prepared with a traditional Neapolitan coffee maker

Cappuccino: equal parts espresso and milk froth

Cornetto: Italian croissant

Succo di frutta: fruit juice

Spremuta d'arancia: fresh-squeezed orange juice

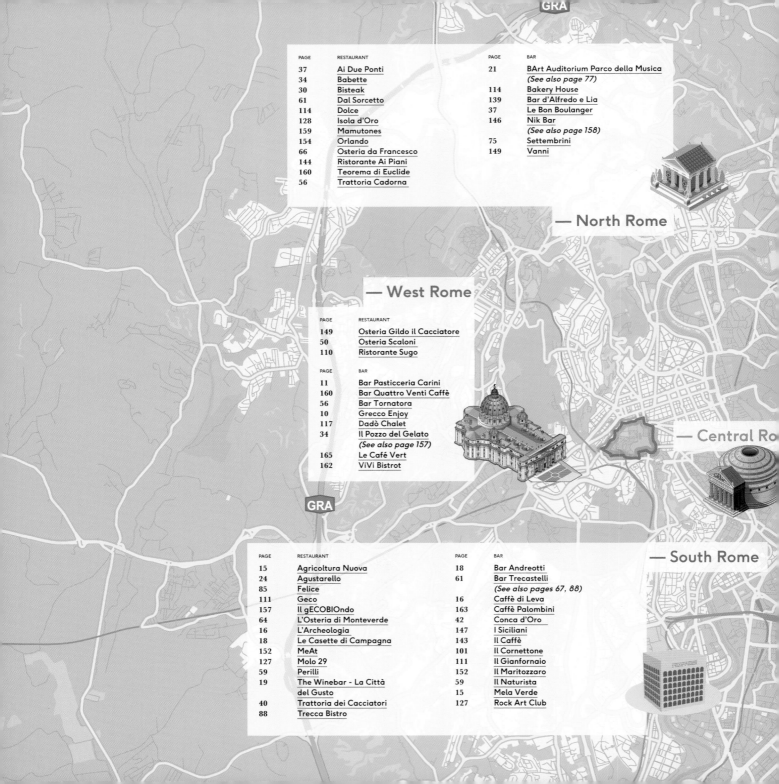

GRA

— North Rome

— West Rome

— Central Ro

GRA

— South Rome

— East Rome

100 LOCALS

Reveal their favorite local secrets

ABOUT THE 100 LOCALS SERIES

We live in a world where every product or service you may want to purchase has already been reviewed online by thousands of satisfied and frustrated clients alike. From a toothbrush to a car, our consumer decisions have never been better informed. Yet, when it comes to travel and leisure in foreign destinations, there is a huge knowledge gap of how the locals live and play.

In this series of crowd-sourced guides of some of the world's most exciting cities, 100 locals share with you their secret spots, their top restaurants, and their favorite social hangouts such as bars, pubs, cafes, clubs, or nightclubs. Savvy travelers may already know some of these recommendations, but most are surprising additions you will be hard-pressed to find on the usual-suspect 'trip advisory' sites.

Packed with curated suggestions of where to hang out, eat, drink, and play in each city, this guide will prod you to venture beyond the epicenter of the metropolis to discover the best-hidden gems known only to the insiders.

The 100 locals are carefully selected to represent a wide cross section of each city's geographic areas, as well as a balanced demographic representation of gender, age, socioeconomic level, profession, and personality types.

Whether you are a seasoned traveler to the featured city, a newbie, or indeed a local, prepare to take the express route to the very core that makes each of the cities in the series a unique destination to visit or live, and as far away as possible from the beaten paths and tourist traps.

ONEHUNDREDLOCALS.COM

OTHER CITIES IN THIS SERIES

NEW YORK CITY
SAN FRANCISCO
LOS ANGELES
AMSTERDAM
BARCELONA
LONDON
SYDNEY
BERLIN
TOKYO
PARIS